T0299821

Gregorio Ballabene's Forty-eight-part Mass for Twelve Choirs (1772)

Neither *Spem in alium*, the widely acclaimed 'songe of fortie partes' by Thomas Tallis, nor Alessandro Striggio's forty-part Mass is the largest-scale counterpoint work in Western music. The actual winner is Gregorio Ballabene, a relatively unknown Roman *maestro di cappella*, a contemporary of Giovanni Paisiello, Joseph Haydn and Luigi Boccherini, who composed in forty-eight parts for twelve choirs. His Mass saw only a public rehearsal and was never performed liturgically despite all of Ballabene's efforts to promote it. On closer inspection, however, the work deserves special consideration as a piece of outstanding combinatory creativity – the product of a talent able to conceive, structure and realise a project of colossal dimensions. It might even be claimed that if Charles Burney had gained knowledge of it, all derogatory comments by nineteenth-century music historians would not have succeeded in extinguishing the interest of later generations. Ballabene's Mass has remained completely unstudied until today, even though the score survives in prominent collections. This study offers, for the first time, a historical and analytical perspective on this overlooked manifestation of a very individual musical intelligence.

Dr Florian Bassani is a lecturer at the Institute of Musicology, University of Bern, Switzerland.

Royal Musical Association Monographs

Series Editor: Simon P. Keefe

This series was originally supported by funds made available to the Royal Musical Association from the estate of Thurston Dart, former King Edward Professor of Music at the University of London. The editorial board is the Publications Committee of the Association.

For more information about this series, please visit: www.routledge.com/music/series/RMA

Gregorio Ballabene's Forty-eight-part Mass for Twelve Choirs (1772)

Florian Bassani

Routledge
Taylor & Francis Group

LONDON AND NEW YORK

First published 2022
by Routledge
2 Park Square, Milton Park, Abingdon, Oxon OX14 4RN

and by Routledge
605 Third Avenue, New York, NY 10158

Routledge is an imprint of the Taylor & Francis Group, an informa business

© 2022 Florian Bassani

The right of Florian Bassani to be identified as author of this work has been asserted by him in accordance with sections 77 and 78 of the Copyright, Designs and Patents Act 1988.

All rights reserved. No part of this book may be reprinted or reproduced or utilised in any form or by any electronic, mechanical, or other means, now known or hereafter invented, including photocopying and recording, or in any information storage or retrieval system, without permission in writing from the publishers.

Trademark notice: Product or corporate names may be trademarks or registered trademarks, and are used only for identification and explanation without intent to infringe.

British Library Cataloguing-in-Publication Data
A catalogue record for this book is available from the British Library

Library of Congress Cataloging-in-Publication Data
A catalog record has been requested for this book

ISBN: 978-1-032-12892-4 (hbk)
ISBN: 978-1-032-12893-1 (pbk)
ISBN: 978-1-003-22671-0 (ebk)

DOI: 10.4324/9781003226710

Typeset in Times New Roman
by Apex CoVantage, LLC

Access the Support Material: www.routledgemusicresearch.co.uk

Note for the Reader
In view of the fact that the source texts in various languages contained in Appendix I of this study are reproduced without the respective translation into English for reasons of space, an additional document has been made available for download on the Routledge Music Research Portal. This document also contains, in addition to the **text documents including the translations**, all **figures** of the volume. Here, especially in the case of the pages of the score manuscript, a free enlargement enables the best possible readability of the musical text.

The document can be accessed via: www.routledgemusicresearch.co.uk. Please enter the activation word **RRMusic** and your email address when prompted. You will immediately be sent an automated email containing an access token and instructions, which will allow you to log in to the site.

For Vasiliki

Contents

Introduction

The golden age of Venetian polychorality may be clearly dated to the last decades of the sixteenth century and the early years of the seventeenth. The zenith in the history of its Roman equivalent was reached much later, around 1650, a flourishing that persisted, albeit with a gradual decrease in popularity, until the 1730s. In Rome, the phenomenon is linked to names such as Antonio Maria Abbatini, Paolo Agostini, Orazio Benevoli, Francesco Berretta, Stefano Fabri, Francesco Foggia, Virgilio Mazzocchi and Giuseppe Ottavio Pitoni, among many others whose works have not survived. Remarkably, most of these names and the outstanding compositions associated with them fell into oblivion after only a few decades – as did the highly refined skills of polychoral composition.

When Charles Burney, during his visit to Rome in November 1770, was shown the score of a newly completed, though most unusual, sixteen-part work by papal singer Pasquale Pisari, he reacted with great astonishment:

> A century or two ago, the author of fuch a compofition would have had a ftatue erected to his honour; but now, it would be equally difficult to find 16 people who would hear it with patience, as that number of good fingers, in any one place, to perform it.[1]

Burney clearly held the work and its author in high regard, yet even though Pisari may have been in the prime of his life and may have occupied a prestigious position, in the Englishman's eyes his considerable talent had come several generations too late: the era of polychoral sacred music had long been a thing of the past. Burney quite rightly states that in former times masters of Pisari's rank would have been showered with honours, but now,

---

1 Burney, *The present state* (1771), p. 371; 2nd edn (1773), p. 383f. For the quotation in its context see Appendix I, Document 1.

DOI: 10.4324/9781003226710-1

neither an audience for such works nor adequate performing forces – the basic preconditions for resuming the great tradition of polychoral practice that spanned a century and a half – would even seem conceivable.

So how can it be explained that only a few years after Burney's memorable encounter (and without his knowledge) another relatively little-known Roman composer, Gregorio Ballabene, had a Mass for as many as forty-eight real parts in twelve choirs performed – and with little chance of ever having 'a ſtatue erected to his honour'? The following book presents this largely unknown, though extremely peculiar, contrapuntal composition and examines its historical context. The aim is to comprehend the role and significance of such a work, which in Western music history occupies a unique position.

1 Twelve-choir performances

With regard to seventeenth- and eighteenth-century Roman festival culture, numerous documentary testimonies provide evidence of liturgical celebrations accompanied by polychoral music. Diaries, diplomatic notes and official accounts of solemn liturgies (especially extant lists of participants) refer to a musical framework of four, six or even eight choirs for special occasions. Among these records, however, performances with a full dozen single choruses are extremely rare. The best-documented case is Agostini's performance with twelve choirs for second Vespers at St Peter's Basilica on 29 June 1628, the patron saints' day. The symbolically arranged ensemble[1] consisted of at least 146 participants.[2]

In the Holy Year 1650, the festivities for St Dominic's Day (then celebrated on 4 August) at the Dominican church of Santa Maria sopra Minerva featured 'twelve choirs of most excellent music' involving 150 performers.[3] A composer is not named; only in later sources is Benevoli (*maestro di*

---

1 The list of participants defines the number of choirs as a reference to the twelve Apostles ('vna muſica a dodici Chori da me Paolo Auguſtini Maeſtro di Cappella . . . in honore de dodici Apoſtoli'); I-Rvat, ACSP, Cappella Giulia 81 (1628), ff. 70–73.
2 Ninety-seven singers (twenty-three sopranos, twenty altos, nineteen tenors, seventeen basses, plus another eighteen unspecified 'Cantori'), twenty-five instrumentalists (one bassoon, five cornettos, seven trombones, seven violins, four viols, one violone), twelve organists and twelve directors, including Agostini himself. There are several notes in the register referring to an unspecified number of extra singers who participated on an honorary basis, waiving their fees; the total number of participants might therefore have been slightly above 146. For a detailed description of this case, including a transcription of the list, see Bassani, *Römische Mehrchörigkeit*, Dokument 1628.
3 '12 Chori d'eccellentiſſima muſica . . . con 150. muſici'; Ruggieri, *Diario*, p. 176. Another source confirms the number of choirs ('per essere l'anno santo hanno fatto una festa straordinariamente bellissima, e solennissima, e fra le altre una musica à dodici cori'; [Anonymous], 'Diario dell'anno M. D. C. L., Libro secondo', I-Rvat, Barb. lat. 4819, f. 102v; cited in Riepe, 'Musik im Anno Santo', p. 109.

DOI: 10.4324/9781003226710-2

cappella at St Peter's) mentioned as the music director at that particular event.[4]

Twenty-five years later, in the same church and on the same occasion, another twelve-choir ensemble was engaged for Vespers, again as an extraordinary musical highlight during Holy Year. This time the music was entrusted to Giovanni Battista Giansetti, *maestro di cappella* of San Giovanni in Laterano, who conducted the enormous ensemble that this time also included a remarkable number of instrumentalists.[5]

The jubilees of 1700 and 1725 seem to have involved smaller performing forces. It was not until 1750 that the *maestro di cappella* at the Vatican basilica, this time Niccolò Jommelli, attempted once more to adorn second Vespers on 29 June with festive music of grander dimensions, now with singers even in the cupola. His list records twenty-one sopranos, eighteen altos, twenty-two tenors, twenty-five basses and another nineteen singers in the dome (five sopranos, five altos, five tenors and four basses), as well as eleven violins, seventeen double basses and twelve organists, plus, in all probability, the eighteen vocalists of the Cappella Giulia (the choir of the basilica). Including Jommelli himself, this is an ensemble of 164 participants.[6]

---

4 Baini in 1828, without any reference, specifies Benevoli as the author of the Mass for twelve choirs performed on that occasion ('a quarantotto voci in dodici cori reali . . . di Orazio Benevoli, cantata da cen[to]cinquanta professori nella chiesa di S. Maria sopra Minerva . . . il dì 4. Agosto del 1650'; Baini, *Memorie*, vol. II, p. 316, n. 636).

5 'La Festa di San Domenico di Suriano fù celebrata . . . con Muſica à 12. Cori, guidata dal Signor Gio: Battiſta Gianſetti celebre Maeſtro di Cappella, con buone voci, e concerti di Sinfonie'; Caetano, *Le memorie*, p. 297.

6 The *Diario ordinario* reports 'more than 200 persons, both voices and instruments, with eleven Organs, and the Echo choir at the Cornice of the Dome' ('di ſopra 200. perſone tra voci, ed iſtromenti, con undici Organi, e l'Eco ſul Cornicione della Cuppola'; *Diario ordinario*, n. 5142, 4 July 1750, p. 17). Another testimony specifies the number as 184 singers and 40 instrumentalists ('1750. 29 Giug.° Nel Secondo Veſpero cantato da Monſig.ᵉ Santamaria con musica solenne, e copioſa da' Musici in Num.ʳᵒ 184., 12. Organi, 12. Violoncelli, 16 Contrabaſsi con Eco alla Cupola, compoſizione del Jommella [sic]'; I-Rvat, ACSP, Cappella Giulia, 426, fasc. 3 [between ff. 15 and 16]). The number of performers is confirmed as 224 also by an official Vatican diary (I-Rvat, Diarii I, 1750 [143]). Concerning the event, see also Heyink, 'Con un coro'.

   It may be attributable to Jommelli's lack of experience in polychoral settings – and also to the fact that by 1750 polychoral music with choirs spaced widely apart was very seldom practiced – that the performance did not satisfy the more demanding listeners. A few days after the event, Girolamo Chiti, *maestro di cappella* at San Giovanni in Laterano, relates to Padre Martini in Bologna that he was told that, in terms of coordination, things did not work out perfectly ('p. quanto mi hanno riferito è andato stentato, e fuori di Battuta'; see Chiti's letter dated 1 July 1750, in I-Bc, Carteggio martiniano, I.12.124).

What all these records have in common is that not a single surviving composition by these figures (Agostini, Benevoli, Giansetti and Jommelli) is known to match this particular ensemble format, and yet, on the basis of these scarce sources, music historiography has passed on these names – especially Agostini, Benevoli and Giansetti – as belonging to the authors of works of near mythical proportions: twelve-choir compositions that nobody has ever seen.[7] How can this be explained?

As a matter of fact, Roman sacred music performances with a large number of choirs are documented with some frequency, but any corresponding repertoire appears to be lost. At the same time, extant performance materials of works for two, three or four real choirs clearly demonstrate that sets of partbooks were frequently copied – obviously in order to double, triple or quadruple a choral texture – to create large-scale polychoral repertoire by adapting existing works to the ephemeral performing forces.[8] By systematically multiplying the number of real parts by means of ripieno choirs (performing at least during defined sections, if not the entire work), even double-choir settings in eight real parts were extended, at times very considerably.[9] The presence of non-real choirs is effectively a universal parameter

---

7 For a still early example of such glorifying records, see Pietro Alfieri's obituary for Pietro Raimondi (1786–1853) in *L'Album. Giornale letterario e di belle arti*, XX (1853), pp. 296–298, in which many of Baini's historical notes on Roman polychorality are handed down (based on Baini, *Memorie*, vol. II, p. 316, n. 636). Alfieri's homage is reproduced, among others, in: Kantner, *Aurea luce*, pp. 232–236. On a legendary forty-eight-part Mass by Agostini see also Ambros, *Geschichte*, vol. IV (1878), pp. 105–106; 3rd edn (1909), vol. IV, p. 136.

8 In this context it may be recorded that various (mainly Italian) authors explicitly refer to the possibility of performing their own works with extra choirs based on a multiplication of the partbooks. See for instance the performance notes in Giacobbi, *Prima parte de salmi concertati* (1609); Fergusio, *Mottetti* (1612); Donati, *Salmi boscarecci* (1623) or Rigatti, *Messa e salmi* (1640), not forgetting Viadana, *Salmi à quattro chori* (1612) and Schütz, *Psalmen Davids* (1619). The method was still common practice in the eighteenth century; see for example the *Salmi a quattro voci* by Modenese *maestro di cappella* Antonio Gianettini (1717).

9 It is noteworthy that in Giansetti's case the extant compositions bearing his name (as well as those mentioned in historical inventories) do not exceed the number of eight real parts in two choirs. The same can be asserted for Jommelli. Only among Agostini's works is a (now lost) *Magnificat a 24 voci* documented, last mentioned in 1931 (Fellerer, 'Verzeichnis': 26 (1931), p. 113). The largest known work by Benevoli is a *Dixit Dominus* for twenty-four real parts in six choirs (partial autograph in I-Rsg, B. 297). There are reasonable grounds to believe that in all the cases of twelve-choir performances described earlier, textures for forty-eight real parts were never performed. In this respect it should be added that the capability to conceive at least sixteen-part textures was an aspiration of many Roman *maestri di cappella* of the time, as a matter of prestige, and even lesser-known figures have left works in exactly this format (among them Angelo Berardi, Vincenzo Bona, Pompeo Cannicciari, Carlo Cecchelli, Antimo Liberati, Alessandro Melani, Paolo Petti, Lorenzo Ratti, Giuseppe De Rossi, Nicolò Stamegna and Giovanni Vincenti).

in polychorality, not only in its Roman manifestation, and a great number of smaller-scale compositions testify to this.[10]

Music research has long neglected the fact that in polychorality what you see in the score as a real-part structure is not necessarily what you hear in performance. The texture in real parts manifests the indispensable, essential core of the work, while its components may be multiplied, depending on the requirements and facilities of the individual event.

---

10 The doubling device plays a significant role among the various technical effects on which polychoral textures rely. How easily the human ear can be deceived through doubling becomes clear when a choral texture of only four real parts is performed in an alternating manner, section by section, by two, three or four spatially dislocated ensembles. When all choirs unite, e.g. in the concluding section, the acoustically enriching effect belies the fact that the sounding texture comprises only four real parts, now 'amplified' in the most simple way. The same experiment may be repeated using a double-choir texture in eight real parts performed section by section by four or six ensembles and so on. For a good example of this phenomenon, from outside the Roman and Italian spheres, see Heinrich Ignaz Franz Biber's *Missa Salisburgensis* (1682) and its various recordings. This work is for eight 'choirs' notated on fifty-three staves, and the choral texture, consisting of sixteen voices, is mostly set in eight real parts and in several passages only four. The instrumental parts move mostly *colla parte* with the vocal parts, and a real fifty-three-part texture is never reached. As experience shows, the acoustical persuasiveness results from the skillful timbral composition of the individual (vocal and/or instrumental) choirs on the one hand and their cleverly designed spatial disposition in performance on the other.

2 The presence of a glorious past

The extant Rome-related polychoral works in real parts only in very rare cases go beyond a four-choir texture. Apparently, compositions for up to six real choirs were written by composers such as Abbatini, Agostini, Benevoli, Berretta, Fabri and Mazzocchi;[1] however, only a handful of twenty- or twenty-four-part works survive, some of them in fragmentary form. These represent examples of extraordinary combinatorial skill and outstanding artistic achievement. The extant large-scale polychoral works and the written testimonies referring to lost ones point to a high point in the history of seventeenth-century Roman music.[2]

During his Italian journey, Burney himself seems to have obtained the score of one of these magnificent works, for years later, in his *General History of Music* (1789), he affirms ownership of a twenty-four-part Mass by Benevoli, a composition 'in which the learning and ingenuity furpafs any

---

1 The posthumous fame of Paolo Agostini (ca 1583–1629) encompasses even eight-choir works, according to Liberati ('e trà le altre fue opere merauigliofe fece fentire nella Bafilica di San Pietro, nel tempo ch' egli vi fù Maeftro di Cappella, diuerfe modulationi à quattro, à fei, & otto chori reali, & alcune che fi poteuano cantare à quattro, ouero fei chori reali fenza diminuire, ò fneruare l'armonia, con iftupore di tutta Roma', Liberati, *Lettera*, f. 27). Moreover, among Roman composers, Baini (1828) lists Asprilio Pacelli as the author of twenty-part motets, also mentioning the no longer extant 'Psalms and motets for four, six and nine choruses by Francesco Berretta' ('Li salmi, ed i mottetti a 4. 6. e 9. cori di Francesco Berretta'; Baini, *Memorie*, vol. II, p. 316, n. 636).

2 The largest-scale compositions among the completely preserved works assignable to this category are the aforementioned *Dixit Dominus . . . A 6 Cori Obligati* by Benevoli (in I-Rsg, B. 297; see Chapter 1, n. 9) and the *Magnificat a 24* (in D-Rp, BH 6299a) attributable to Virgilio Mazzocchi. For an edition of the first, see Benevoli, *Psalmus*; for an edition and analysis of these and several similar compositions, see Bassani, *Römische Mehrchörigkeit*, vol. III.

DOI: 10.4324/9781003226710-3

thing of the kind that has come to my knowledge'.[3] In fact, by Burney's time the stylistic principles of concerted music had long been established all over Europe, and Roman polychorality started to enjoy popularity among intellectual music lovers abroad. While in Berlin in the 1780s, German composer Johann Friedrich Reichardt presented to his colleagues a four-choir Mass by Benevoli, newly acquired during his first visit to Italy (1783),[4] thereby awakening the interest of connoisseurs and inspiring Carl Friedrich Christian Fasch to compose a real sixteen-part Mass of his own (1783), to be performed in 1791 by the newly founded Sing-Akademie. As a significant element of the then current German (not exclusively Berlin) zeitgeist, the secular interest in polychoral sacred music – both ancient and modern – was still being cultivated a generation later, as reflected in works such as Felix Mendelssohn's four-choir motet *Hora est jam nos de somno surgere* (1828) and, even later, as in Peter Cornelius's *Cum sanctis tuis* (1848) for four choirs and four organs and the sixteen-part a cappella Mass that Eduard Grell (1800–1886), then director of the Berlin Sing-Akademie, first performed in 1861.[5]

At the time of Burney's travels, in the Rome of 1770, some of Benevoli's, Berretta's and Pitoni's polychoral works were still part of the traditional festive music repertoire at St Peter's.[6] But these aside, hardly anybody still composed

---

3 Burney, *A general history*, vol. III (1789), p. 525. For the quotation in its context see Document 8. At an earlier point of his *General history*, Burney had already mentioned the work briefly ('I am at preſent in poſſeſſion of the Maſs by Benevoli, in twenty-four parts, for ſix choirs . . . and a movement for twelve ſopranos, or treble voices, of equal extent'; ibid., vol. II (1782), p. 474).

4 The work has been identified almost certainly as Benevoli's *Missa in diluvio aquarum multarum* (Scheideler, *Komponieren*, p. 282ff).

5 This monumental work (a score of 235 pages, comprising all movements of the Ordinary) entitled *Missa sollemnis senis denis vocibus decantanda* was published in Berlin in 1863 (ed. Bote & G. Bock; two differently engraved versions, same plate number: 5658). A partial manuscript copy of the work, dated 1880, is extant in D-DT; in D-B there are also excerpts from a sixteen-part *Deutsches Hochamt* by Grell, dated 1845. At this point it might be anticipated that, as director of the Sing-Akademie, Grell knew Ballabene's Mass, not only from the Sing-Akademie's library but also from a partial performance abroad, as he explained to a journalist in 1886; see Wichmann, 'Das größte Musik-Kunststück', p. 1131. For the quotation see Chapter 11, n. 25. Concerning the extraordinary phenomenon of a secular polychoral music culture in nineteenth-century Berlin, including an analysis of the previously mentioned works, see Scheideler, *Komponieren*, p. 143ff. For a more general perspective on the phenomenon of the Protestant revival of Giovanni Pierluigi da Palestrina and his contemporaries in music centres in Germany, see Garratt, *Palestrina*, pp. 62–132; regarding Grell's *Missa sollemnis*, ibid., pp. 128–131.

6 In 1775 the Cappella Giulia was still paying copyists for preparing the materials (mainly partbooks) for important festal occasions, among them copies of polychoral works; see for example I-Rvat, ACSP, Cappella Giulia, 195 (Entrata e vscita della ven. Cappella Giulia, 1765–1796, p. 229; 9 December 1775): 'A Gius.ᵉ Lorenzini Archiviſta dell'Archivio di

or performed polychoral music. At any rate, Burney's amazement was certainly real when he was shown Pisari's sixteen-part manuscript. As a composer himself, he was familiar with the enormous challenges of counterpoint:

> I never faw a more learned or ingenious compofition of the kind. Paleftrina never wrote in more than eight real parts, and few have fucceeded in fo many as thofe; but to double the number is infinitely more than doubling the difficulties.[7]

Yet he reveals a kind of helpless perplexity in the ensuing statement,

> This work . . . though it may be thought by fome to require more patience than genious to accomplifh, feems fufficient to have employed a long life in compofing, and to entitle the author to great praife and admiration.

Anyone who has ever tried to conceive a musical texture of, say, only eight real parts (even if homophonic) will be able to gauge the immense compositional challenge implied by Burney's remark that 'to double the number is infinitely more than doubling the difficulties' and to comprehend the high esteem in which outstanding exponents such as Agostini, Mazzocchi or Benevoli were held by their contemporaries. Burney's account in fact crystallises the basic dilemma that characterises a substantial part of the present study – which is on the one hand an assessment and appreciation of the undeniable technical achievement of creating a contrapuntal work consisting of an unprecedented number of real parts but on the other hand is an account of the difficulties involved for the retrospective observer attempting to locate this achievement historically and artistically. Burney's possibly spontaneous reaction to call for a memorial to the author of such a feat may be regarded as an expression of the puzzlement and disconcertedness with which such highly sophisticated creations inevitably confront the observer – and posterity in particular. This applies all the more to works which, as in the case of Pisari's composition, were already behind the times at the moment of creation.

As far as Pisari is concerned, his compositions appear to have been relatively well known and sought after abroad. In the 1770s, the Portuguese

---

S. Gio: in Laterano Scudi Undici m.^{ta} p. copie di tre Mefse à 16 c[onformement]e al suo Conto et da sua ric.^{ta} sc. 11'.

7 Burney, *The present state* (1771), pp. 370–371; 2nd edn (1773), pp. 383–384 (see also Document 1). What Burney did not know is that Palestrina actually left a small number of works in twelve real parts.

minister in Rome, on behalf of the Crown, 'ordered from him a *Dixit for* 16 *parts* in four real choirs, plus the music for all services [i.e. the Propers] of the year, for 4 parts and organ', as Giuseppe Baini reports.[8] A first version of the work had been composed at least five years earlier, around 1770/1771, but it was not until spring 1776 that the score was presented to Giambattista Martini (1706–1784). The Bolognese Franciscan friar, the leading authority of his time in the field of sacred music, highly appreciated the work. He even paid supreme tribute to the composer in asking to receive Pisari's portrait for his picture gallery.[9] Baini furthermore affirms, 'Fr Martini, on seeing his compositions, said that he did not know many composers who approached the style of Palestrina more than Pasquale Pisari did, and that he could rightly call himself the *Palestrina of the eighteenth century*'. Unfortunately, Pisari's talent had little time to flourish: 'Right after having sent all the music to Lisbon in two chests, poor Pisari in the flower of his manhood passed away in 1778'. He was around 53 years old.[10]

8 'La corte di Portogallo per mezzo del Ministro in Roma gli richiese un *Dixit a* 16. *voci* in quattro cori reali, e tutto il servigio per l'annuale a organo a [sic] 4. voci'; see Baini, *Memorie*, vol. II, p. 65, n. 513. For the quotation in its context (including the passages that follow) see Document 12. It should be noted that Giuseppe Baini (1775–1844) relates the entire event without indicating his sources. When making these observations, published in 1828, Baini was chamberlain of the pontifical chapel. As a counterpoint scholar of Giuseppe Jannacconi (1741–1816), he clearly stood in the Palestrinian tradition of the 'Scuola romana', and in his role as administrator of the chapel he was also in charge of conserving the glorious memory of the institution. The episode on Pisari (in other sources also 'Piseri') is obviously part of the more recent narrative of the chapel's history.

9 For Pisari's presentation letter dated 17 April 1776, together with the draft of Martini's reply (27 April), see I-Bc, Carteggio martiniano, I.030.048 and I.030.048a. With the help of Luigi Antonio Sabbatini, one of Martini's principal Roman correspondents, the portrait was delivered at the beginning of September that year (I-Bc, Carteggio martiniano, I.016.087, I.016.088, I.016.091, I.016.092, I.030.049). The painting is still part of the picture gallery of the Bolognese Museo internazionale e biblioteca della musica (I-Bc, Iconoteca, B 11814 / B 39124; www.bibliotecamusica.it/cmbm/scripts/quadri/scheda.asp?id=198). As early as summer 1771 Sabbatini had informed Martini about the existence of a sixteen-part *Dixit Dominus* by Pisari and about the composer's aim of bringing it to Martini's attention (see Sabbatini's letter of 8 July 1771 in: I-Bc, Carteggio martiniano, I.016.071). It remains unclear whether this is the same work as the one referenced later: in his letter to Martini of 5 August 1775, Sabbatini newly talks about 'a sixteen-part Dixit he [Pisari] is making just now' ('un Dixit à 16 che stà facendo adeſso'; I-Bc, Carteggio martiniano, I.016.073); its dispatch is announced on 10 April 1776 (I-Bc, Carteggio martiniano, I.016.083). There is reason to suspect that Pisari wrote only one sixteen-part *Dixit Dominus*, in 1771, which five years later (presumably in a revised form) he sold as a specially commissioned production to the Portuguese court (see n. 10).

10 Pisari is assumed to have been born in 1725. He died around 18 March 1778, the date on which Sabbatini informs Martini (I-Bc, Carteggio martiniano, I.016.117); on 25 April, Sabbatini asks Martini to write a eulogy; on 15 May he confirms receipt (I-Bc, Carteggio

Earlier on, in autumn 1776, Pisari's patron had provided for a public pre-view of the work, and so, to continue with Baini, 'The *Dixit* was rehearsed in the church of the Holy XII. Apostles, at the behest of the Portuguese minister, who was very pleased with it'. Of particular interest is what fol-lows in parentheses:

> (on that occasion, one hundred and fifty performers having been invited, they also rehearsed the *Kyrie* and *Gloria* in 48 parts divided into 12 choruses, a work by Gregorio Ballabene, a Roman, to which Fr Martini offered his *elaborate endorsement* in print).[11]

It is striking to see a notice of this kind confined to a side note, as if it were an unimportant secondary comment (all the more as Baini on another occasion praises the same Mass as 'A truly golden work' and 'worthy of veneration'; see Chapter 10, n. 13). Considering solely the extraordinary number of parts in Ballabene's work, Baini's statement about it appears fairly reserved compared with his interest in Pisari's *Dixit Dominus*. We will return to Baini later.

martiniano, I.016.119 and 120). The obituary in the *Antologia romana*, IV (1778), p. 400, wrongly indicates 27 March as the date of Pisari's death.

While the Mass for four choirs mentioned by Burney has not yet come to light, the sixteen-part *Dixit Dominus* has been handed down in several sources. The score and part-books that are still extant in Lisbon (P-Lf, Ms 172/22) are most probably the autograph materials Pisari sent to the Portuguese court in 1777/1778. For nineteenth-century copies see D-Mbs, Mus. MS 999 and 2959, A-Wn, SA.67.G.16 MUS MAG and D-MÜs, SANT Hs 3210. Laurence Feininger made an edition of the work in 1961 (see Chapter 3, n. 5). Feininger mentions further copies in D-B (Mus. MS T 198; Mus. MS 17547), D-Dslub (Mus. MS 3127/D/1) and D-Rp, which all at present cannot be detected.

Considering that the sixteen-part *Dixit Dominus* by Pisari preserved in Bologna (I-Bsf, MS FN.P.I.8) represents the same work as do the previous sources, it is most likely that the work submitted to Martini in 1776 was effectively the *Dixit* that Pisari sent to Lisbon a year later. This might explain why Pisari, after having dispatched the score destined for Bologna, heavily insisted that Martini did not let it out of his hands, for whatever reason, as relayed by Sabbatini to Martini on 11 September 1776 ('mi prega il Sig.ʳ Piseri che l'avvisi acciò che il Salmo a 16 voci che gli mandò non eſca dalle sue mani à coſto di qualunque impegno gli poteſſe giungere'; I-Bc, Carteggio martiniano, I.016.093), with the request repeated on 21 September (I-Bc, Carteggio martiniano, I.016.094).

Further support is lent to this interpretation by the fact that the *Dixit Dominus* manu-script in I-Bsf shows a striking concordance with other Pisari autographs. I am grateful to Dr Carlo Vitali in Bologna for his advice regarding the historical background of the document.

11 Baini, *Memorie*, vol. II, p. 65, n. 513. For the quotation in its context see Document 12.

3 Burney's 'Mass'

The manuscript that Pisari presented to Burney on Friday 16 November 1770 is quite likely to have been nothing other than his *Dixit Dominus* – and not, as Burney recalls, 'a maſs' in sixteen real parts. As mentioned earlier, a sixteen-part *Dixit* by Pisari did exist in 1771, when the composer undertook a first trial for submission to Martini for his opinion. This work can be identified as Pisari's only known four-choir composition, and no other polychoral works of his are otherwise documented, in copies, in inventories or in any further testimonies. From his hand, not even works for twelve real parts are recorded. With the historical decline of polychoral music culture in mind, to which Burney clearly refers, it seems perfectly possible that Pisari during the course of his career wrote only one sixteen-part composition at all, as early as 1770, the year of his presentation to the highly amazed English music historian. Supposedly, it was the very same work that five months later Pisari almost sent to Martini, and it does not take much to imagine that in the following years, through an acquaintance with the Portuguese minister to the Holy See, Pisari came to sense his big chance in life: the opportunity to make himself known to the Portuguese court through a series of outstanding achievements in his field. In 1775, Pisari announces that he's writing – again, this time officially – a sixteen-part *Dixit Dominus* that is soon to be dispatched to Martini.[1] In that sense it would appear only logical that, on the eve of the 1776 performance at the Roman church of Santi XII. Apostoli, Pisari would seek to ensure at any price that Martini should not leave the manuscript in other hands: the padre had received the work a few months before, yet in the meantime Pisari had offered it to Lisbon as a

---

1 Seen in a wider framework, the fact that on 5 August 1775 Sabbatini in Rome spreads the news that Pisari's '<u>Dixit</u> à 16' is being composed 'just now' (see Chapter 2, n. 9) almost appears to be part of some sort of plan of disinformation. It is quite conceivable that Pisari was basically reworking the score he had created years earlier.

DOI: 10.4324/9781003226710-4

'custom-made product' for the Crown – and as a precious foundation stone for his own career.[2]

The fact that Pisari, according to Baini, worked hard during this period and 'within months . . . tirelessly accomplished the immense work' (i.e. the '*Dixit for* 16 *parts* in four real choirs, plus the music for all services of the year', ordered by the minister) – alongside the other elements of the scenario surrounding this work's creation – demonstrates that Pisari was about to reach an important turning point in his professional life; in early 1778, when his Lisbon connections were sounder than ever, he had even been under discussion as successor to the vacant *maestro di cappella* position at St Peter's.[3] Thus it is not hard to imagine the profound sense of loss his colleagues must have felt at his sudden death in March that year.

It should be noted that Pisari's *Dixit Dominus* fits surprisingly well Burney's description of the reputed 'maſs in 16 real parts', as it is in fact 'full of canons, fugues, and imitations'. He continues:

> In the compoſition of Signor Piſari, every ſpecies of contrivance is ſucceſsfully uſed. Sometimes the parts anſwer or imitate each other, by two and two; ſometimes the ſubjects are inverted in ſome of the parts, while their original order is preſerved in others.

Pisari does not set the text in the seventeenth-century 'concertato alla Romana' manner, in which every verse is given a different musical setting, with new melodic and rhythmic material as well as varying metres and in which differing combinations of voices are deployed.[4] His musical transformation of the psalm is entirely through-composed (similar to Pitoni's handling of the genre). In a densely woven texture, every verse of the biblical text is performed by the full four-choir ensemble, and thus the work is divided into few, extremely long sections in which, to quote Burney again, 'every ſpecies of contrivance is ſuccefsfully uſed'.[5]

2 In this regard it appears noteworthy that the subtitle 'Anno Jubilej 1775' seems to occur only in the eighteenth-century manuscript in Bologna (I-Bsf, FN.P.I.8) as well as in several nineteenth-century copies of the work (in D-Mbs, D-MÜs and A-Wn) but not in the one in Lisbon.

3 See the corresponding allusions in Sabbatini's letter to Martini from 7 March 1778 (I-Bc, Carteggio martiniano, I.016.116).

4 For a description of the phenomenon see Dixon, *Concertato alla romana.*

5 For the modern edition see Pisari, *Psalmus.* Apart from the overall perspective of the contrapuntal texture, the 82-page modern score gives an idea of the enormous dimensions of the work (in fact, Burney recalls a composition 'of a very conſiderable length'; see

In light of other, similar memory lapses he commits, Burney may be forgiven for remembering Pisari's work as 'a maſs'. In his *General History of Music* he claims to possess 'ſeveral curious productions of this kind, by Benevoli', compositions he most probably purchased during his visit to Rome in 1770. These examples allow him, he writes,

> to affirm, that his [Benevoli's] powers of managing an unwieldy ſcore are truly wonderful; particularly in a maſs *a ſei cori*, or twenty-four voices, in which the learning and ingenuity ſurpaſs any thing of the kind that has come to my knowledge.

Furthermore, he owns 'another maſs of his compoſition, for twelve *ſoprani*, or treble voices, in conſtructing which, the nearneſs of the parts muſt have augmented the difficulty of avoiding confuſion'.[6]

When Burney died, his library was sold, and the only polychoral works by Benevoli listed in the auction catalogue are: 1. a sixteen-part Mass, 2. a twenty-four-part *Dixit Dominus* and 3. a twelve-part motet (all in parts, no score).[7] The two pieces described earlier ('a maſs *a ſei cori*, or twenty-four voices' and 'another maſs . . . for twelve *ſoprani*') seem to be the *Dixit* and the motet mentioned in the catalogue; Burney's term 'Mass' apparently refers to a 'sacred vocal work' in a more general way.[8] On the other hand, the first of the three Benevoli works offered at the auction may correspond to one that Burney describes in another of his studies (in 1785), where it is transfigured by Benevoli's legendary greatness:

> On the ceſſation of the plague at Rome, in the early part of the laſt century [sic], a maſs compoſed by Benevoli, for ſix choirs, of four parts each, was performed in St. Peter's church, of which he was maeſtro di capella; and the ſingers, amounting to *more than two hundred*, were

Document 1), which greatly extends the seven psalm verses in musical terms (doxology and 'Amen' alone spread over almost twenty pages). For important similarities, especially in terms of structuring a polychoral setting without solo sections, some of Pitoni's settings of the same psalm words provide an excellent basis for comparison (see Pitoni, *Psalmus Dixit Dominus, II*, and Pitoni, *Psalmus Dixit Dominus, III*).

6 Burney, *A general history*, vol. III (1789), p. 525. For the quotations in their context see Document 8.
7 *Catalogue of the music library of Charles Burney*, p. 10, lot nos. 228 and 229.
8 This also applies in a letter Burney wrote to German scholar Christoph Daniel Ebeling in 1772, in which this same terminology appears in exactly the same context (see Document 2).

arranged in different circles of the dome: the ſixth choir occupying the ſummit of the cupola.[9]

The tale of the Mass with the choirs 'arranged in different circles of the dome' clearly refers to Benevoli's *Missa in angustiis pestilentiae* (1656/1657), though in a somewhat enchanted and exaggerated guise.[10] It may be that the four-choir Mass by Benevoli that Burney owned was just this work. With regard to the other two Benevoli compositions mentioned in the auction catalogue (and in the *General History of Music*), an even more specific assertion can be made, as Benevoli's only twenty-four-part work known today is in fact a *Dixit Dominus* for twenty-four real parts in six choirs; his only extant composition for twelve sopranos is the antiphona *Regna terrae*, also in six choirs.

More intriguing still is that all three of these works have been documented in the Lateran music archive at least since the 1750s.[11] All this would seem to suggest a common provenance for Burney's copies of the works.[12] The Englishman maintained excellent relationships with prominent figures on

---

9 Burney, *An account*, Preface, p. VIII. The event had already been mentioned earlier, in Burney's *General history of music*, where he refers to 'the ſcore conſiſting of twenty-four different parts' (Burney, *A general history*, vol. II (1782), p. 11). According to the auction catalogue, at his death at least, Burney did not possess the score but only the partbooks. However, the edition of the work published in London in 1848 is, according to the editors, based on 'an Italian MS. score, formerly in the possession of Dr. Burney' (Bishop and Warren, *Repertorium*, p. [II]). The location of this source (and of all the other polychoral works from Burney's estate) is currently unknown.

10 In his transmission of the same legend to Ebeling he continues, admitting: '& tradition says the effects produced by such a number of parts reinforced by so many voices was [sic] beyond description & imagination'; see Document 2.

11 *Missa tempore pestilenti[a]e* (I-Rsg A. 288a); *Dixit Dominus Domino meo 2.ᵈⁱ Toni | del Sig.ʳ Oratio Benevoli. Vaticano | Fatto a 24 Voci | cioè | A 6 Cori Obligati* (I-Rsg, B. 297); *Regna terr[a]e | A 12 | Canti Obligati | di Concerto | Oratio Benevoli | Mott.º p. ogni tempo* (I-Rsg, B. 2117). For the historical presence of these documents in the holdings of the archive, see the handwritten catalogue compiled in 1754 (I-Rsg, Inventario II A), pp. 83, 40, 103. For an edition and analysis of the Benevoli *Dixit Dominus* and the motet *Regna terrae*, see Bassani, *Römische Mehrchörigkeit*, vols. I and III.

12 The same applies to the other two Roman polychoral works, a Mass by Paolo Petti and another Mass by Lorenzo Ratti, mentioned in *Catalogue of the music library of Charles Burney*, p. 11: '287 *Petti* (P. P.) Messa, Kyrie, &c. a 4 Cori in Score [MS]'; '288 *Ratti* (L.) Do [i.e. Messa], Kyrie, &c. do. d. o.' (i.e. 'a 4 Cori in Score [MS]') – here, the letters 'd' and 'o' mean 'ditto'. In both cases the still extant manuscript copies in I-Rsg (in these cases sets of partbooks) are also documented in the handwritten 1754 catalogue (signatures: I-Rsg, A. 291 and I-Rsg, A. 354).

the Roman music scene, among them members of the papal chapel. The 'supply routes' of these goods therefore seem obvious.

Burney's enthusiastic description of the Benevoli 'maſs *a ſei cori*, or twenty-four voices, in which the learning and ingenuity ſurpaſs any thing of the kind that has come to my knowledge' and that of the 'maſs . . . for twelve *ſoprani*, or treble voices, in conſtructing which, the nearneſs of the parts muſt have augmented the difficulty of avoiding confuſion' seem to be based on sets of partbooks only: in the auction catalogue the two pieces (as well as the sixteen-part Mass by Benevoli) are reported exclusively in this source form. If Burney had no score compiled from these parts, his idea of the compositional structure would have been on the speculative side, based on his intuition rather than on a more sound knowledge of the work.[13]

---

13 In view of this, it is possible to understand why Burney states the following with respect to the twenty-four-part setting and the movement for twelve sopranos: 'There can be little melody in any of theſe multiplied parts; but to make them move at all, without violation of rule, requires great meditation and experience'; see Burney, *A general history*, vol. II (1782), p. 474. The two polychoral Masses in his collection by Petti and by Ratti, both in score, may have added important insights to Burney's vision of polychoral textures, which in the end led to his fervent appraisal.

4 Ballabene and his Mass in Martini's correspondence

In his previously mentioned note on the rehearsal of Pisari's *Dixit Dominus*, Baini only briefly mentions the other composition presented on that occasion, 'the *Kyrie* and *Gloria* in 48 parts divided into 12 choruses, a work by Gregorio Ballabene'. Later generations of music historians similarly provide very little information on both the author and his work. Any attempt to get closer to this mysterious composition would first have to consider the extant copies of the score, which have survived in several prominent collections. Second, it is important to examine the correspondence that accompanied Ballabene's numerous efforts to promote the work and to obtain official appreciation of its qualities. In the present study, these and further source materials are taken into consideration, thus revealing additional details about the score and the history of its transmission.

The earliest known record pertaining to Ballabene's Mass is dated 15 August 1772, the day when the Roman *maestro di cappella* submitted it to Martini. In the accompanying letter (Figure 4.1) Ballabene uses florid words to depict himself as an undiscovered mastermind whose work is the object of scorn and derision to the music world, and to his Roman colleagues in particular, who consider it 'a prank, an imposture'. In an imploring tone he begs Martini to scrutinise his 'petty production' in order to determine its 'merits, or demerits'[1] and to express his approval in an official manner, in order to publicly defeat his enemies and help him advance his career. The writing ends with Ballabene even hoping that Martini might support him in

---

1 'Sono Stato costretto a Sentire da più d'uno di questi Maestri di Cappella, e da varj avtorevoli Dilettanti, efsere vna Buffonata, vn'Impostura; che le Voci Sono Solamente quattro; che queste Composizioni Sono giuochi, e Simili galanterie . . . acciochè ed io, e gli altri restiamo illuminati, [. . .] Sopra il merito, o demerito della mia meschina produzione'; I-Bc, Carteggio martiniano, I.030.053. For the quotations in their context see Document 3.

DOI: 10.4324/9781003226710-5

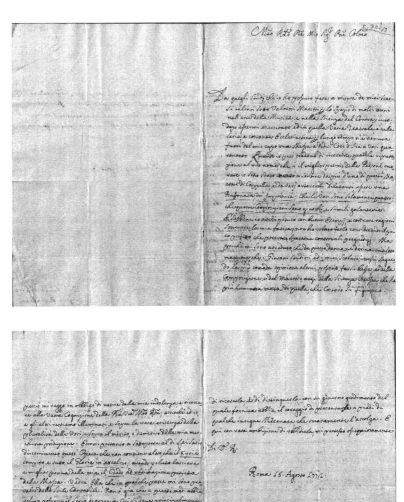

Figure 4.1 Letter from Gregorio Ballabene (Rome) to Giambattista Martini ([Bologna]), dated 15 August 1772: Ballabene's first attempt to bring his Mass to Martini's attention.

Source: I-Bc, Carteggio martiniano I.030.053. For the transcription see Document 3.

finding some prominent patron ('qualche insigne Mecenate') to make his star rise with a gesture of public recognition.[2]

The postal consignment was accompanied by another letter from Rome, likewise dated 15 August, signed by Cardinal Alessandro Albani (1692–1779), who presents the forty-eight-part composition as 'a work by a dependant of mine' ('un'opera fatta da un mio Dipendente'), asking Martini to state his opinion on it and to assess if he considers it practicable.[3] The latter aspect is evidently one of the main points of critique as far as Roman experts were concerned.

From another letter from Ballabene to Martini, dated 11 November 1772, it emerges that Martini in the meantime has replied to the cardinal in order to invoke further support for the composer.[4] In the same letter, Ballabene newly insists (though indirectly) on receiving official approval from the Bolognese Accademia Filarmonica, on whose board Martini played a leading role (at the time, he was serving as 'Secondo Definitore': second assessor).[5]

In July of the following year, 1773, Cardinal Albani wrote to Martini with a request from Ballabene that the score of his Mass be returned.[6] Martini immediately replied that he would comply, even though he had assumed that the score had been presented to the academy with no need for restitution. He announces dispatch, informing his correspondent that the score is very large

---

2 Ibid.

3 I-Bc, Carteggio martiniano, I.015.051. Albani, nephew of former pope Clement XI, had already emerged as a patron of the arts and sciences in earlier years, with beneficiaries such as Giovanni Battista Piranesi, Pietro Metastasio, Niccolò Jommelli, Johann Joachim Winckelmann and Anton Raphael Mengs. The background of the relationship between Ballabene and the cardinal is unclear.

4 I-Bc, Carteggio martiniano, I.030.054. For another short reference in this regard, see Albani's letter to Martini dated 7 November 1772; I-Bc, Carteggio martiniano, I.015.053. Relations between Martini and Alessandro Albani, cardinal since 1721, can be traced back to at least 1761 (see I-Bc, Carteggio martiniano). In the 1770s, the cardinal was Protector of the Collegio di San Bonaventura, the college of the Order of Friars Minor Conventual (OFM Conv) in Rome, residing at the headquarters of the order, at the church of Santi XII. Apostoli. In this function he was an important point of contact for Martini with the Holy See. The reigning pope, Clement XIV Ganganelli (1705–1769–1774), was, like Martini, a member of the OFM Conv. Santi XII. Apostoli had been Ganganelli's titular church during his time as cardinal-priest (1762–1769), and his tomb was transferred there in 1802, years after his death.

5 I-Bc, Carteggio martiniano, I.030.054. Martini's title is explicitly indicated in Martini, *Descrizione*, p. XV (see also Document 4). As will be seen, Ballabene himself had been a member of the Philharmonic Academy of Bologna since 1754 and therefore already knew Martini from earlier years. All the more reason to be surprised by his repeatedly impetuous tone.

6 'Defiderandola l'Autore, che me ne fà premurose istanze'; I-Bc, Carteggio martiniano, I.015.054.

and also that he – confidentially – wishes to communicate to the cardinal some of his concerns regarding the matter.[7] Only later does he relay his critical notes to Ballabene. On 28 August, Ballabene thanks Martini for having returned the score to him at the cardinal's request, but again he does not tire of emphatically demanding academic recognition of his work.[8]

Soon after, on 4 September, Martini replied in his usual matter-of-fact style, referring to a number of minor contrapuntal errors in the composition that would have to be corrected before an approbation could be expressed. At the same time, he reprimands the Roman *maestro di cappella* for his impatient attitude. On elimination of all errors and receipt by Martini of a corrected copy of the score, the approval and commendation would immediately be granted by the academy.[9]

In his response (15 September), Ballabene seems to have felt the need to defend his impatience, using his reputation and employment status as excuses. Instead of showing humility, which might appear appropriate to the situation, he even begs for understanding regarding the compositional errors, pointing out that such a complex texture necessarily demands certain licences. He even asks that Martini signalise the errors requiring elimination. Despite all this, Ballabene declares himself disposed to carry out Martini's demands, 'as my esteem depends solely on this Mass and on your approval', adding also that 'dependent on this esteem is some better sustentation for myself and my family', thereby even further lamenting his fortuneless professional career.[10]

Replying on 2 October 1773, Martini does not dwell on Ballabene's lamentations, limiting his observations instead to the indispensable corrections. What Ballabene has tried to cover up as unavoidable 'licences' are quickly unmasked by Martini as intolerable faults – especially where parallel fifths and octaves are concerned. Martini in clear terms admonishes the composer to distinguish indubitably between licences and errors, for the sake

7 'Di esporle confidentem.^te alcune mie difficoltà'; I-Bc, Carteggio martiniano, I.015.054a. As the courier encountered problems in delivering the item, a further short interchange of messages took place (I-Bc, Carteggio martiniano, I.015.055 and I.015.055a); on 21 August 1773 the cardinal confirmed the arrival of the package in Rome (I-Bc, Carteggio martiniano, I.015.056).

8 I-Bc, Carteggio martiniano, I.030.056.

9 I-Bc, Carteggio martiniano, I.030.057.

10 'Sono pronto ad ubbidire ogni di Lei Comando, e mutare qualunque cosa Ella mi additerà, poichè la mia Stima dipende vnicam.^e da queſta Meſsa, e dalla Sua approvazione; e da questa stima dipenderà ancora qualchè migliore Sostentam.° p. me, e p. la mia Famiglia; giachè finadora viuo aſsai ristrettam.^e e Sono meno considerato di que' Maeſtri, che si fanno aſsai compatire anche nelle Composizioni à quattro Voci.'; I-Bc, Carteggio martiniano, I.030.058.

of preserving the honourability of the academy, the composer and Martini himself. In conclusion, he emphasises once again that as soon as the corrections are done the approbation will be issued.[11]

Ballabene obeys and sends a corrected score. Even though Martini confirms its arrival on 3 November, announcing that the approbation is forthcoming,[12] another impatient request by Ballabene, dated 8 January 1774, newly challenges Martini's composure.[13] In his immediate response (11 January) he assures Ballabene that the approbation is on its way, and that if there are any Roman colleagues still resistant to recognising the Mass's value and significance, they will be defeated when comparing the work with the great polychoral compositions still known in Rome – works 'for 3, 4, 5, 6 and 8 choirs' by Agostini, Benevoli and other great masters of the past. Moreover, he encourages him to plan a performance of the work in order to convince all remaining doubters.[14]

In a short note of 22 January 1774, Cardinal Albani thanks Martini for having sent (on 15 January) the approval for the two Mass movements by Ballabene ('l'attestato in favore delli <u>Kyrie</u> e <u>Gloria</u> del Sig.^r Ballabene'), without providing any further information.[15] Soon after having received the official recognition, Ballabene, on 26 January, combines his expressions of gratitude with yet another request for Martini's assistance in improving his career situation but without specifying exactly the type of support required.[16]

In his reply (now lost), Martini must have honoured Ballabene with the invitation to send his portrait to add to his picture gallery of outstanding musicians. With the following letter (12 February 1774), Ballabene – still in an overly exaggerated manner – expresses his gratitude as well as intimating that Martini's request should be announced publicly, as Ballabene is fearful that he will otherwise gain a reputation for being bold and overly ambitious.[17]

---

11 I-Bc, Carteggio martiniano, I.030.059.
12 I-Bc, Carteggio martiniano, I.030.055. On this occasion Martini tells Ballabene that Giuseppe Ottavio Pitoni (1657–1743) had also attempted to write a similar work, leaving it unaccomplished. In his draft letter he even adds – but later on cancels – that Pitoni's work was 'not composed with that observance of the Principal Rules which are compatible with a commitment of such great difficulty' ('~~non composto con quella ofservanza delle Principali Regole che sono compatibili con un impegno di tanta difficoltà~~'). It seems that Martini was tempted to show some enthusiasm about Ballabene's work but then had second thoughts.
13 I-Bc, Carteggio martiniano, I.030.063.
14 I-Bc, Carteggio martiniano, I.030.064.
15 I-Bc, Carteggio martiniano, I.015.057.
16 I-Bc, Carteggio martiniano, I.030.061.
17 'Perchè io non riceva una taccia di ardito e di troppo ambizioso'; I-Bc, Carteggio martiniano, I.030.060.

When Ballabene, on 17 August, informs Martini that he is about to dispatch the portrait, he seizes the opportunity again to deplore his miserable fate in Rome 'with a very large family and without any advantage from all my efforts'.[18] Again, there is no documented reply from Martini.

On 29 August 1774 Cardinal Albani again thanks Martini for his helpfulness in the matter and for having shared his opinion regarding the Mass. He also returns to his former concern, uttered more than two years previously,

Figure 4.2 Unknown artist, portrait of Gregorio Ballabene, made upon invitation by Martini (undated oil painting [1774]).

Source: I-Bc, Sala Bossi, inventario B 11917 / B 39253.

---

18 'Con numerosa Famiglia, e senz'alcun profitto di tante mie fatiche'; I-Bc, Carteggio martiniano, I.030.062. The portrait must have been ready for delivery two months earlier, as emerges from a letter Sabbatini wrote to Martini on 25 June 1774 (I-Bc, Carteggio martiniano, I.016.049); see also Sabbatini's notes in this regard from 10, 20 and 23 August 1774 (I-Bc, Carteggio martiniano, I.016.051, I.016.052 and I.016.053). Like Pisari's, Ballabene's portrait is still part of the Bolognese Museo della musica (Figure 4.2). For the picture gallery and its history, see also Degli Esposti, 'La Galleria'.

as to whether or not Martini considers the composition realisable in practical terms.[19] Evidently, there remained the key issue of a public performance.

The rather long period of *sede vacante* between the death of Pope Clement XIV (22 September 1774) and the election of his successor, Pius VI (15 February 1775), seems to have been one of the reasons for an interruption in the correspondence regarding Ballabene's case. In the meantime, however, the approbation, dated 11 January 1774, had appeared in print. On 25 November 1775, more than a year after the last exchange of letters, Ballabene contacted Martini one more time. By this point he had presented the Mass to the new pope, reporting, 'His Holiness was infinitely pleased to receive it and has exhibited spirit both to hear it and to award it'.[20] But again, according to the composer, the wicked voices at court were cursing the work and denouncing it as unperformable, without even having seen it. Ballabene is convinced that the printed approbation has proved insufficient and consequently begs Martini to help him find a way to get the work publicly performed.

As far as a performance of the Mass is concerned, Martini replies on 6 December 1775, saying that even just the singers of the Cappella Pontificia and those of the two chapels at St Peter's and at the Lateran should be sufficient; brought together with vocalists from other chapels, the number would be considerable. In this letter, however, Martini avoids making any further proposals, but promptly contacts Cardinal Albani once more to ask for his support in this matter (probably also in financial terms).[21]

---

19 I-Bc, Carteggio martiniano, I.015.058.
20 'Sua S.tà l'ha gradita infinitam.ᵉ, ed ha mostrato genio e di sentirla, e di premiarla'; I-Bc, Carteggio martiniano, I.030.065.
21 I-Bc, Carteggio martiniano, I.030.066. The undated draft letter to the cardinal is written on the same sheet.

5 The 'rehearsal' and its outcome

Based on Ballabene's correspondence with Martini (which ends in December 1775), it remains unclear when the eagerly awaited performance of Pisari's *Dixit Dominus* took place, followed – according to Baini – by Ballabene's Mass. In nineteenth- and twentieth-century literature, 1770, 1774 and 1777 are indicated, with no exact dates given, whereas contemporaneous records of the event are almost entirely missing. The whole event seems to have passed without any wider public attention: neither the *Gazzetta universale*, nor the *Antologia Romana*, nor the Roman *Diario ordinario* (in which even events of minor significance are reported) took notice of the 'rehearsal' organised specifically for the two fairly unusual works.

The only concrete evidence is given by Roman *maestro di cappella* Luigi Antonio Sabbatini (1732–1809), who from the 1760s on maintained a lively correspondence with Martini. Sabbatini was not only Martini's brother monk (OFM Conv) but also his scholar, and he served at the Roman church of their order – the church of the Holy XII. Apostles. In his letters he frequently refers to Ballabene and Pisari, almost as if he were an intermediary, apparently attempting to acquire Martini's support for Pisari as a composer. In a letter dated 21 September 1776, he incidentally mentions that 'on Thursday 26 in our church the rehearsal of Mr Piseri's sixteen-part Psalm will take place, there will be Cardinal Albani and other sovereignties'.[1] What follows, however, seems to be in reference more to Ballabene's Mass than to the *Dixit Dominus*: 'The same [i.e. Cardinal Albani] has been consoled very much by your letter, of which many copies were made'.[2] It can be assumed that there was no need to publicly defend Pisari's work

---

1 'Giovedì 26 del Corrente nella noſtra chieſa si farà la prova del Salmo à 16 del Sig.ʳ Piseri, che v'interviene il Sig.ʳ Card.ᵉ Albani ed altri Sig.ʳⁱ'; I-Bc, Carteggio martiniano, I.016.094.
2 'Il med.º è rimaſto molto conſolato della sua lettera della quale ne sono state fatte molte copie'. Ibid.

DOI: 10.4324/9781003226710-6

with the help of Martini's approval, considering the fact that (according to Baini) it had officially been commissioned by the Portuguese court. Sabbatini's intimation therefore appears rather to reflect the ongoing campaign in favour of Ballabene's intent to gain official recognition for his Mass. From 1772 onwards, Cardinal Albani had actively advocated for Ballabene, and he seems effectively to have been one of the leading forces (besides the Portuguese minister) behind the performance initiative. As mentioned earlier, the cardinal was closely tied with the college of the order, which was part of the convent, and this again may explain the choice of location.[3] On the other hand, the fact that Sabbatini was the *maestro di cappella* of the church seems to have played no significant role: by all accounts, he was not actively involved in the event.

In any case, it remains surprising that Sabbatini's note to Martini regarding the performance mentions not a word about either the Mass or its author. It might be tempting to think that all of the people involved were tacitly allowing the obstinate Ballabene (who, after all, must have been considered a pain in the neck, a tiresome busybody, not only by Martini and Sabbatini but also by Albani) to have his way and get public recognition, whatever the outcome of the entire initiative.

The event on 26 September 1776, a Thursday, was presumably made possible as a kind of joint venture between the cardinal and the minister. Each of the two (relatively short) pieces of music, owing to their extraordinary nature, would have justified public performance, but the financial expense would have outweighed the effect. The customary sponsorship of an entire festive liturgy (in Roman practice consisting of first Vespers, Mass and second Vespers) would have contributed much more to the cultivation of the patron's image than would a single 'test demonstration' of an unknown work that out of context promised considerably less public attention. In reference to the event, in fact, the word 'concert' is not used anywhere: Sabbatini explicitly calls it a 'rehearsal' ('prova'), a term used also by Baini (1828) when referring both to the sixteen-part *Dixit* by Pisari and to Ballabene's Mass.

---

3 See Chapter 4, n. 4. The Portuguese national church Sant'Antonio dei Portoghesi was presumably excluded for its much smaller size. As only sacred music was to be presented, a church may in any case have seemed an appropriate venue; however, symbolic significance aside, no secular space (e.g. the Salone of the Archiginnasio della Sapienza, the great hall of the German College or the Sala degli Orazi e dei Curiazi of the Palazzo dei Conservatori on Capitoline Hill) would have been sufficient in size for the forces involved. Nonetheless, the fact that the number of the Apostles is the same as the number of choirs in Ballabene's Mass seems to have been the result of a curious coincidence rather than being of any intended emblematic significance, unlike Agostini's Vespers for twelve choirs at St Peter's in 1628 (see Chapter 1, n. 1).

Therefore, it is obvious that the exercise was intentionally held in a semi-official and undefined atmosphere, open to the public and placed apart from all significant liturgical events of the season. As a matter of fact, the feast of St Francis on 4 October, more than a week later, was celebrated at Santi XII. Apostoli with the customary effort, 'with magnificent decoration and music', including the presence of several prominent cardinals at Mass, many members of the nobility and a great number of people.[4]

Concerning Pisari's and Ballabene's works, however, there is no other context in which a setting of *Dixit Dominus* (Psalm 110, the first of between five and seven psalms sung at Vespers) and a *Kyrie* and *Gloria* (the first two out of six elements of the Mass Ordinary) could possibly appear in combination, if not in an experimental preview-like concert rehearsal. Aside from that (and despite the economic aspect), a far more important reason for desisting from any 'official' performance of these works in a liturgical context, unless it was preceded by an intensive rehearsal period, is the fact that the practical challenges involved in both cases could hardly be overestimated.

On the one hand, it is more than likely that the sixteen-part polyphonic texture by Pisari, if performed by professional Roman chapel singers of medium-high proficiency, would have turned out successfully even in a sight-read run-through.[5] On the other hand, the far more complex texture of Ballabene's forty-eight-part Mass movements, although structured largely in binary metre (apart from *Kyrie* II, the sections 'Domine Deus', 'Quoniam' and 'Amen', all in 3/2), would have made coordinating the enormous ensemble problematic.[6] As is evident in the case of Jommelli's ambitious festive music at St Peter's in 1750 (see Chapter 1, n. 6), there are reasons to assume that mid- to late eighteenth-century Roman performers were no longer sufficiently familiar with the technical requirements and effective challenges of polychoral coordination practices, especially when a large number of dislocated ensembles was involved.[7] In this sense, Burney's appraisal,

4 'Con nobile apparato, e mufica nella Bafilica de' SS. XII. Apoftoli dei PP. Min. Conventuali, nella quale vi fi portarono a celebrare la S. Meffa diverfi ragguardevoli Ecclefiaftici, ed alla vifita gli E.mi Sigg. Cardinali Carlo Rezzonico, ed Archinto; e sì in quefta . . . Chiefa . . . il concorfo della Nobiltà, e Popolo è ftato affai numerofo'; *Diario ordinario*, n. 186 (12 October 1776), p. 4. As Cardinal Albani is not mentioned, it can be assumed that this was an event entirely different from the 'rehearsal'.

5 To gain an idea of the challenges in terms of performance practice and especially ensemble coordination, see the score edition of the work (Pisari, *Psalmus*).

6 For a first general impression regarding the essential melodic and rhythmic features within the full twelve-choir texture, see *Kyrie* I, especially the concluding section (Figure 5.1, Figure 7.2).

7 For seventeenth- and early eighteenth-century performance practice standards see Bassani, 'Polychoral performance practice'.

stating that in the 1770s it was difficult to find adequately competent vocalists to perform such repertoire, appears well grounded.

If it is true that 'one hundred and fifty performers' were gathered (as stated by Baini), the twelve-choir texture could have been realised with roughly three singers to a part.[8] In terms of spatial disposition of the choirs, modes of conducting and the number of organs involved, we do not know how Pisari and Ballabene organised the event. Technically speaking, the options for displaying the performers, whether in four choirs or in twelve, would have been numerous, and most probably different solutions were adopted for the two pieces.

As far as the outcome of the test performance of Pisari's *Dixit Dominus* is concerned, the Portuguese minister 'was very pleased with it' (Baini). In reference to Ballabene's *Kyrie* and *Gloria*, however, collective memory seems to orientate towards an icy silence. The fact that there is not a single documented opinion, neither positive nor negative (apart from the composer's enthusiastic self-testimony, as will be seen), may indicate that things did not turn out in the best possible way.

At the same time, the sponsorship of the event by prominent and powerful authorities, a fact of which all – performers and listeners alike – must have been aware, may have been the reason why a failure of any kind would have been discreetly concealed. Baini, who hardly hesitated in criticising music-related issues of the past (his Palestrina biography is aptly named *Memorie storico-critiche*), did not even articulate an opinion or report any historical note regarding the outcome of the performance of Ballabene's music. When his study was published in 1828 he was *camerlengo* (general administrator) of the papal chapel, in which post – and as Palestrina biographer in particular – he was responsible for cultivating remembrance of Roman sacred music history. His silence on the matter seems to reflect that in all official memories handed down to him this aspect of the musical past had been successfully erased. The fact that not only in print media – such as official gazettes, anthologies or diaries – but also in Martini's and Sabbatini's correspondence a cloak of silence seems to be have been laid over

---

8 The number of 150 performers can be found in several other testimonies of large-scale polychoral performances in seventeenth- and eighteenth-century Rome. It can be presumed that it reflects more or less the number of professional singers present in the church chapels of the city. In a 1694 count, 158 singers in 25 chapels were documented (Mischiati, 'Una statistica'). In 1708, a tax-related assessment lists 154 professional Roman singers in 17 chapels, without taking account of the boy sopranos, supposedly several dozen, still in education (Barbieri, 'An assessment'). The previously mentioned document regarding the performance Jommelli directed at St Peter's in 1750 (see Chapter 1, n. 6) refers to 184 participating vocalists. The scale of 150 performers in 1776, as given in Baini's records, therefore seems plausible, at least in terms of availability.

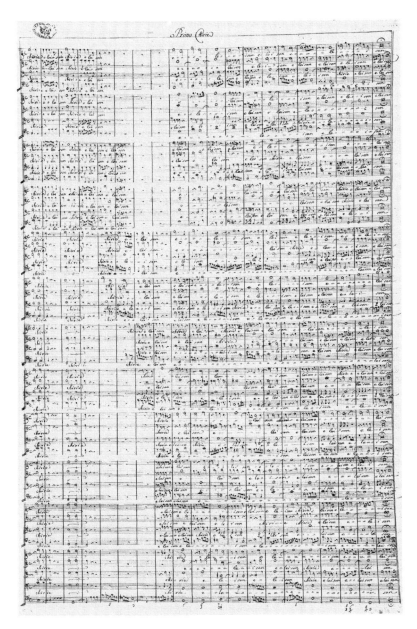

Figure 5.1 Gregorio Ballabene, *Messa a dodici cori, Kyrie* I ('Primo Chirie'), I-Rama, A. MS. 316, f. [1ᵛ].

anything regarding Ballabene's Mass after its performance may support this interpretation.[9]

Whatever the outcome was, due to the participation of most of Rome's chapel singers (and presumably the presence of a number of curious *maestri di cappella*), the performance must have left a lasting mark on Ballabene's standing on the local music scene. Only from a nineteenth-century French review does it emerge that rumours of a suboptimal impression had in fact circulated ('the effect was obscure, confused, and . . . the entrances of the various motifs could not be distinguished'), thus affecting the reputation of the work in the long term.[10]

As discussed, various factors make it difficult to imagine that Ballabene's colossal composition went smoothly at its first rendition. It can be assumed that basic issues of coordination would have arisen, as fundamental skills familiar to any maestro, chapel singer and organist, such as establishing the beat or switching to a different metre, may have been unpredictably difficult to execute. In the multiplied dimension of this exceptional event and given the relevant spatial and acoustical components, a straightforward procedure could easily have turned into an extraordinary challenge, all the more so in a forty-eight part contrapuntal texture. Experience suggests that such core problems can be overcome through intense and systematic rehearsal, something that in the present case was most probably not possible.

It should be stressed at this point that the composition is not full of treacherous chicanery and conceited artfulness. The complex texture may very well be performable, but it is worth highlighting that even for an ensemble consisting only of professionals a single sight-reading rehearsal – in this case, half a rehearsal – would hardly have been sufficient to achieve

---

9 Only in 1784 are the author, his work and Martini's defence briefly recalled, in a memory by Martini from which still no bitterness or disdain seems to emerge (I-Bc, Carteggio martiniano, I.029.007a; for the quotation see Chapter 10, n. 4).

10 For the 1853 contribution by François-Joseph Fétis (1784–1871), which at least partly coincides with Baini's narration in terms of content, backed up supposedly by oral tradition and thus wrongly reporting certain aspects of the event (including Burney's presence and testimony), see Document 14. The basic essence of this account is reflected in Fétis's biographical article on Ballabene, published years earlier, in which he also stresses that 'much larger masses of singers would have been necessary' ('D'ailleurs des masses chantantes beaucoup plus considérables auraient été nécessaires pour rendre sensibles les entrées des parties de chaque chœur'; Fétis, *Biographie universelle*, vol. II (1835), p. 49; 2nd revised edition, vol. I (1860), p. 231). The posthumous edition of August Wilhelm Ambros's *Geschichte der Musik* (1878) joins in with the sober remark that the Mass 'was performed . . . with dubious success' ('wurde . . . mit zweifelhaftem Erfolg aufgeführt'; Ambros, *Geschichte der Musik*, vol. IV (1878), pp. 117–118).

convincing results. Under the circumstances, the undeniable qualities of the work (which are discussed later) could not have been adequately demonstrated. For these reasons, on 26 September 1776 the audience almost inevitably would have obtained an unsatisfactory overall impression.

It remains unknown where exactly the outcome of Ballabene's presentation was located on a scale that has a 'brave run-through' as the best-case scenario (possibly after repeated attempts) and a 'disastrous failure' as the worst. One point, however, is clear: a triumph for the author and his work would have left clearer traces, at least as far as press and eyewitness accounts are concerned. Moreover, one may assume that in the event of success, the composer would have received positive attention from the music scene – whereas the opposite seems to have been the case.

6 Consequences for Ballabene's professional advancement

As far as Ballabene's career is concerned (his own ambition being the main driving force for promoting the work to the public), the desired launching effect that the rehearsal at the church of the Holy XII. Apostles was supposed to have failed to materialise.

Only a few key facts are known about Ballabene's life preceding the events surrounding his Mass. It is not even clear where and when he was born, but as his name is often associated with the attribute 'Romano' he was probably of Roman birth. His family roots seem to lie in the upper Papal States (in the current Emilia Romagna and Marche regions), where the surname is still quite common today and where Ballabene spent a significant part of his professional life.

There is no information about his musical education, but as a youth he was already active as an organist (see Document 7b). His earliest known work, a Christmas cantata, carries the year 1737.[1] From the early 1740s onwards, his name appears in the confraternity archives of the Roman Congregazione di Santa Cecilia.[2] In 1746 he served as assistant to the *maestro di cappella* Luigi Besci at the church of Madonna dei Monti. His first known carnival opera *Il marchese del Bisogno*, a 'farsetta in musica', was staged in Rome in 1752, at the small Teatro de' Granari, near Piazza Navona.[3] In the early 1750s and certainly by June 1753, Ballabene and his family left Rome for Macerata.[4] In a 1754 autograph letter from Macerata he desperately

---

1 Manuscript copy in I-Bsf, FN.B.I-1.
2 First mentioned in the minutes of the general assembly dated 18 July 1741; see I-Raanc, 'Verbale della congregazione generale'.
3 Printed libretto in P-Cug, Misc. 569, Nº 9547.
4 In a letter from Fulgenzio Morichi (Rome) to Martini (Bologna), dated 16 June 1753, Ballabene is mentioned as 'M.ro di Cappella in Macerata' (I-Bc, Carteggio martiniano, I.002.003). His earliest known work traceable to this place is a *Pastorale del signor abbate Pietro Metastasio da cantarsi nella chiesa della Confraternita delle Sacre Stimmate della città di Macerata la notte del S. Natale l'anno 1753* (printed libretto in I-MAC, B.C.MC 7.7. B.102).

DOI: 10.4324/9781003226710-7

bemoans his professional state and the humiliation to which he is subjected in that city ('with a wife and 5 children'; 'all these things never happened in the 40 years I lived in Rome').[5] In the same year, he became a member of the Accademia Filarmonica di Bologna.[6] During Carnival 1755 at the Macerata theatre his version of Metastasio's *Catone in Utica* was given.[7] Also in 1755 he applied for a *maestro di cappella* position (presumably at the Duomo) at Urbino.[8] In 1757 he set another libretto by Metastasio, *L'eroe cinese*, this time for Carnival at Fabriano (Teatro de' Nobili).[9] In summer 1759, 'Gregorio Ballabene di Terni' is among the twenty applicants for a *maestro di cappella* position at Orvieto (supposedly at the cathedral).[10] In the printed libretto of the oratorio *S Francesco di Sales* from 1760 Ballabene is mentioned as *maestro di cappella* at Gubbio, a post he supposedly

5 'Con Moglie, e 5. figli'; 'tutte cofe non mai Succefse in 40. anni che hò vifsuto in Roma'; Gregorio Ballabene, autograph letter from Macerata to an unidentified recipient, dated 24 August 1754 (A-Wn, Autogr. 7/9–1). According to this indication, Ballabene would have been born around 1714 (not 1720, as commonly assumed). In which case, the date in the manuscript catalogue entry 'Ballabene Gregorio | Romano nato nel 1741' in the Fondo Baini at I-Rc may perhaps be interpreted as an error in which the numbers have been rotated (see I-Rc, Index de Re Musica, f. 15r).

6 For his admission in January 1754 he submitted a four-part vocal fugue ('Generatio haec prava et perversa', in I-Baf, capsa III, n. 91). In the files held by the academy, apart from the admission year, he is furthermore registered as Roman born, but no year of death is indicated (Gambassi, *L'Accademia*, p. 109, 420). Regarding the admission process, see also Rostirolla, 'La corrispondenza', p. 248. In an autograph letter from Macerata, directed to an unnamed clergyman (most probably Martini in Bologna) and dated 2 March 1754, Ballabene expresses his gratitude for having just received the formal appointment (D-B, Mus. ep. Ballabene, G. 1).

7 Printed libretto in I-MAC, B.C.MC 7.5 B.9.

8 In a two-page letter dated 6 September 1755 he informs Martini about his decision to run for the position ('di concorrere alla Cap[pel]la vacante di Urbino') and asks for his support in the matter. For the document (current owner unknown) see Liepmannssohn, *Katalog* (1886), p. 38; Stargardt, *Die Autographen-Sammlung* (1906), p. 263; idem, *Autographen* (1926), p. 65; idem, *Autographen* (1927), p. 5; Hoepli and Oppermann, *Autographen-Sammlung* (1934), p. 70.

9 Printed libretto in I-Vgc, ROLANDI ROL.0149.13. In the booklet he is referred to as 'Maeftro di Cappella d'Apiro', presumably meaning the Abbey church at Apiro, between Fabriano and Macerata.

10 Letter by Pasquale Antonio Basili at Orte to Martini (1 August 1759) in I-Bc, Carteggio martiniano, I.017.0193. As Basili reports, he and Ballabene had received the same amount of votes, but Basili was preferred although Ballabene was considered 'higher of age and [also] in terms of valuable features' ('che era maggiore d'età, e di requifiti'). Basili furthermore thanks Martini profusely for his reference letter ('il suo atteftato'). A month later the chapel master post at Terni was vacant (letter by Basili to Martini, dated 5 September 1759, in I-Bc, Carteggio martiniano, I.017.0195).

held for several years.[11] An autograph *Compieta a quattro voci concertata* is dated 1762 (I-Bc, DD.110), and a collection of motets with instruments (I-Rc, MS MUS 5679) dates from 1764. Several string quartets in Ballabene's hand (in I-Rc, I-Rsg and I-Rrostirolla) bear the year 1769. These and an orchestral overture (in D-Dl) suggest that he may actually have been a talented violinist.

Further biographical details are missing, until 15 August 1772, when Ballabene, now in Rome again, contacted Martini to promote his twelve-choir Mass. It is unknown at which Roman church he was at that time serving as *maestro di cappella*, but as a member of the Congregazione di Santa Cecilia (as can be ascertained for the period between 1741 and 1797), his institutional career seems to have been characterised by ups and downs and only discreet success. Remarkably, it was only in 1775, a year after Martini's approbation and after 34 years of membership, that Ballabene (at about 60 years of age) was elected to an office within the congregation.[12]

It was hoped that the public rehearsal of the Mass in September 1776 would be a turning point in Ballabene's career; and yet, his employment situation following the event remains unknown. To stay afloat he still had to teach in various minor institutions, such as the Collegio Liegese.[13] Evidently, he continued to depend on occasional commissions, as revealed

---

11 Printed libretto in D-B, Mus. Tb 145. Gubbio is also the place of publication of a libretto for Baldassare Galuppi's popular opera *Li tre amanti ridicoli* (libretto: Ageo Liteo, i.e. Antonio Galuppi), whose dedication speech to a local noblewoman is signed by Ballabene. The performance at Gubbio's Teatro della Fama de' Nobili during Carnival 1765 was apparently under his direction (copy in US-Wc, ML48 [S3471]).

12 In 1775 Ballabene became 'Esaminatore' (I-Raanc, 'Verbale della congregazione generale', 10 May 1775) but failed in the elections of the 'Guardiano dei maestri di cappella' in the following year, which, significantly, took place only weeks after the rehearsal of his Mass on 26 September (I-Raanc, 'Verbale della congregazione generale', 28 November 1776). Only in 1780 does he sign himself officially as 'Eſaminatore de' Maeſtri di Cappella della Congr. dei Muſici di Roma' (see his *Approvazione* dated 18 November 1780, in: Catalisano, *Grammatica-armonica*, p. XXIII; see furthermore Catalisano's letter to Martini, dated 30 October 1780, in which Ballabene is also mentioned among the 'maeſtri di Cappella eſaminatori di Roma', in: I-Bc, Carteggio martiniano, L.117.040). His name is present in the meeting minutes of the congregation as late as 27 July 1797; see I-Raanc, 'Verbale della congregazione segreta'. For notes regarding his institutional career see also Giazotto, *Quattro secoli*, vol. II, p. 19.

13 From a 1779 letter of recommendation (Document 7a–b) it emerges that in earlier years Ballabene had taught at this small institution (also called Ospizio D'Archis, situated in Via dell'Arancio, near Borghese Palace), a college for students from Liège, and that some of his scholars there had even obtained reputable positions in their home town. One of Ballabene's students at the college was Henri-Philippe Gérard (1760–1848), who in his later years taught under the directorships of Méhul and Cherubini at the Paris Conservatoire; Lade, 'Gérard'.

by a sequence he composed in 1778 for the Augustinian nunnery of Santi Quatuor Coronati in Rome.[14] During this period he ran for several important *maestro di cappella* positions: in 1778 at Sant'Antonio in Padua and at San Pietro in Vaticano and in May 1779 at the Duomo in Milan. None of these candidacies was successful.

Regarding the Milan case, it is documented that Ballabene, armed with recommendations from Cardinal Albani and convinced of his artistic excellence, decided to present himself through a notarially certified list of his merits rather than in person. The attestation stresses the following:

> his main reputation procured for him a Mass for forty-eight parts distributed in twelve choirs, which was examined at length by the famous Fr Martini, and by the reputable Bolognese academy, who desired to preserve a copy among the rarest items, furthermore placing a portrait of the author among the most illustrious men of this art.
>
> This Mass was rehearsed in Rome in the church of the Holy XII. Apostles in the presence of the Most Eminent Cardinal Alessandro Albani and countless people who applauded it in full voice. The appraisal can be gleaned from the printed sheets enclosed, published as a sign of gratitude by one of the most excellent scholars of Ballabene.[15]

One may presume that Ballabene's reputation and the fame of his main work on the Italian music scene was not fully congruent with the composer's own assessment. What is certain is that his candidacy for the Milan Cathedral post, together with that of two other contenders (who also had decided not to take on the long and expensive journey), was ruled out at the first selection stage.[16]

---

14   Manuscript copy in D-MÜs, SANT Hs 290. The work with the initial words *Lumen mundi erexit* in Fortunato Santini's copy bears the following preliminaries: *Sequentia quatuor vocibus | In festo S. Augustini Ecclesiae Doctoris | pro Monialibus SS. Quatuor | Coronatum de Urbe | Auctore Gregorio Ballabene Romano | 1778.*

15   For the declaration in its context see Document 7a–b.

16   For the the subsequent course of the proceedings concerning the eight remaining applicants, especially for Martini's detailed vote, see Torri, 'Una lettera inedita'.

7 Martini's approbation

The reference in Ballabene's self-portrayal earlier to 'the printed sheets enclosed, published . . . by one of the most excellent scholars of Ballabene' almost certainly alludes to the preliminary note by Giuseppe Heiberger preceding Martini's approbation in printed form (Figure 7.1).[1] From this *Lettera di Giuseppe Heiberger Romano* it emerges that Heiberger, himself a member of the Bolognese Accademia Filarmonica, was effectively

---

1 Both documents (respectively dated Rome, 5 February 1774; Bologna, 11 January 1774) were published as a single booklet of sixteen pages, entitled *Lettera di Giuseppe Heiberger Romano Accademico Filarmonico che ferve di preludio alla Defcrizione, ed approvazione fattafi dall'Accademia de' Filarmonici di Bologna ad una composizione musicale a 48. voci del signor Gregorio Ballabene maeftro di cappella Romano* (Roma: A. Casaletti, 1774). Heiberger's *Lettera* is set out over pp. III–VI, followed by Martini's *Descrizione, e approvazione dei Chirie, e Gloria in excelsis del signor Gregorio Ballabene compofta in mufica a 48. voci in dodici cori* on pp. VII–XV (for the latter see Document 4). A digital reproduction of the entire document is available at www.bibliotecamusica.it/cmbm/scripts/gaspari/scheda.asp?id=814. In the extant archival materials in Milan (I-Mfd) the booklet mentioned in Ballabene's 1779 candidacy ('the printed sheets enclosed') is missing. It might be added that the *Lettera di Giuseppe Heiberger* does not describe 'the effect of the forty-eight-voice Mass in the rehearsal that had been made of it', as Fétis reports in 1860 ('Joseph Heiberger, musicien allemand fixé à Rome, a fait imprimer dans cette ville, en 1774, une lettre concernant l'effet de la messe à quarante-huit voix, dans l'essai qui en avait été fait'; Fétis, *Biographie universelle*; quotation present only in the 2nd revised edition, vol. I (1860), p. 231). The *Lettera*, which appeared in print more than two years before the 1776 rehearsal, refers exclusively to information relying on the score, as does also Martini's *Descrizione*. Fétis's statement regarding the impact of the work in performance ('notwithstanding a perfect execution, the effect was obscure, confused', words he puts in Burney's mouth; see Document 14) must be based on as-yet-unidentified testimonies.

DOI: 10.4324/9781003226710-8

Figure 7.1 Giuseppe Heiberger, *Lettera di Giuseppe Heiberger Romano Accademico Filarmonico che serve di preludio alla Descrizione, ed Approvazione fattasi dall'Accademia de' Filarmonici di Bologna ad una composizione musicale a 48. voci del signor Gregorio Ballabene Maestro di Cappella Romano* (Roma: A. Casaletti, 1774); title page and beginning of Martini's *Descrizione* (p. VII).

Ballabene's scholar, and it is hardly surprising that in his short introduction the Mass is placed in the best light imaginable.[2]

2 To date, there is little available biographical information about Heiberger. In 1773 he was accepted as a member of the Bolognese Accademia Filarmonica, as revealed by his correspondence with Martini and Antonio Mazzoni, who in 1773 was Principe dell'Accademia (I-Bc, Carteggio martiniano, I.030.074–I.030.079). Heiberger was admitted to the Roman Congregazione di Santa Cecilia in 1774. Giambattista Casali (1715–1792), *maestro di cappella* at the Lateran, informs Martini on 2 July 1774 that Heiberger's admission has made the academy subject to mockery (I-Bc, Carteggio martiniano, I.021.034), specifying only later (22 December 1776) that the candidate on that occasion had cheated in the examination by submitting works by others as his own (I-Bc, Carteggio martiniano, I.021.037). If this had happened earlier, Martini would hardly have accepted Heiberger to introduce his printed approbation of the Mass. According to the *Gazzetta universale* (no. 14, 18 February 1777, p. 115), Heiberger 'Romano' (i.e. of Roman birth) is the author of the newly composed opera *Il colonnello*, performed at the Teatro delle Dame, one of the leading Roman opera houses (also known as the Teatro Alibert). This notification is confirmed by the *Diario ordinario*, which hardly ever reports about opera productions and even extols the highly successful debut of the 'young virtuoso' ('Virtuoso

Martini's discourse on the other hand provides a clearly structured and impartial critical assessment. Starting his observations from the historical phenomenon of counterpoint in general and briefly switching to that of polychoral textures in particular, Martini then directs the attention to Ballabene's work.

Following the principles of polychoral composition, every chorus in this setting has its own functional bass, as Martini points out given the sheer number of twelve individual bass lines. He also appreciates Ballabene's intelligent choice of subjects for the fugues, appropriate for manifold contrapuntal handling. His premeditated approach to inversion, response, tonality, imitation and so on are regarded by Martini as evidence of a far-sighted composer who knows how to retain variety and interest, considering the huge number of parts and the concomitant multiple entrances of the subject. He underlines Ballabene's coherence in respect to resolution of dissonant suspensions – especially those in more than one part at a time – and his artifices in processing them correctly, avoiding unisons and consecutive octaves.

First and foremost, however, Martini highlights that Ballabene distinguishes himself from masters such as Mazzocchi, Valentini, Cifra, Benevoli 'and many others' with his extraordinary ability to write in a texture that goes beyond sixteen real parts without allowing any single part to go in unison with any other. While even these great composers tolerate such licences, Ballabene consistently adheres to the underlying structure of forty-eight independent lines, managing 'to preserve and to exactly maintain the real diversity of the parts'.[3]

What follows at this point of Martini's discourse is of particular relevance, as the arbitrator now draws the reader's attention to the only other work ever written for twelve real choirs: an experiment by Pitoni. In 1753, ten years after Pitoni's death, Martini was shown the manuscript of the work. What he remembers is a texture in forty-eight parts in which the composer had allowed 'several

Giovane'; *Diario ordinario*, no. 222, 15 February 1777, p. 11). Surviving works by Heiberger are mainly of a sacred nature (in D-MÜs, I-Rsg), suggesting further activities as a church *maestro di cappella*. The *Diario ordinario* in fact mentions him in 1776 as having directed festive music for the confraternity at the church of Madonna del Buon Consiglio in the Rione Monti (*Diario ordinario*, no. 140, 4 May 1776, p. 10). Surprisingly, there is no record of him in the extant archive holdings of the Congregazione di Santa Cecilia, a possible result of the shameful circumstances surrounding his admission. Heiberger was probably born around 1750, and he died in Rome in spring 1816. His will reveals that he ended life in absolute poverty at the Ospedale San Michele a Magna Ripa (for the document, dated 31 January 1816 and opened on 21 March 1816, see I-Rasc, Archivio urbano, Sezione 22, Protocollo 81, 21 March 1816). This circumstance is also reflected in the copy of his motet *Sacerdotes Domini* (in D-Mbs, Coll. mus. Max. 161), which bears the anonymous caption 'By Joseph Heiberger . . . [who] died among the aged of San Michele a Ripa, poor, old, miserable, abandoned' ('Di Gius.ᵉ Heiberger . . . morto fra li vecchi di S. Michele a Ripa, povero, vecchio, miserabile, abbandonato').

3 'Confervare, e mantenere efattamente la reale diverfità delle Parti'; Martini, *Descrizione*, p. XI. For the most significant passages of Martini's statement, see Document 4.

of them to sing in unison, now with these, now with those parts of the other choirs'.[4] Ballabene's work, on the other hand, does not rely on this licence.

As Martini emphasises, Ballabene's writing is also striking in terms of textural structure. In passages in which the choirs alternate, he avoids setting the responses in the same key, instead choosing the fourth, the fifth and even the second, the third, the sixth and so on, and in imitation of double counterpoint, the upper and lower choirs at times change position as they respond to one another, in order to create the greatest possible variety, something that (as Martini points out) is among the principal challenges in a twelve-choir setting. For this reason as well, in the alternating sections Ballabene usually has two choirs enter simultaneously, rather than single ones, which helps to keep the passages relatively short.

'Exceptions and licences' that Ballabene adopts and that are given Martini's full approval are consecutive octaves, fifths or unisons that occur as passing quavers. Apart from this rather negligible feature, Martini lists a contrapuntal licence that at the same time is also a stylistic device, frequently applied in seventeenth-century polychoral writing: the so-called Mula. In Ballabene's Mass it is used in *Kyrie* II and at the end of the *Gloria*, where all twelve sopranos are unified in cantus-firmus-like progressions in long sustained notes.[5] Technically speaking, in these moments of the setting the forty-eight parts are considerably reduced in number, but the desired effect clearly strengthens the character of the closing section of the movement.

In terms of licences, Martini briefly discusses the necessity of skipping single words of the text here and there in order to facilitate the movement of the parts, and he underlines Ballabene's need to incorporate some of the leaps that would not have been tolerated under any circumstances in classic counterpoint, neither ascending nor descending: these are all uncommon intervals such as augmented fourths, major sevenths and those exceeding an octave, exceptions granted obviously only in conditions of absolute necessity. The truth is, however, that in the tutti sections of Ballabene's work, melodic progressions in which, for instance, leading notes in cadential clauses are resolved by a leap down a major seventh, or in which fancy

---

4 'Che varie di eſſe cantaſſero in uniſſono, ora con alcune, ora con altre Parti degli altri Cori'; Martini, *Descrizione*, p. XIf.

5 This highly effective compositional medium was described generations earlier in Pitoni's *Guida armonica* and named 'tener la Mula'; Pitoni, *Guida armonica*, p. 27 (for the related passage in the manuscript version of the treatise see I-Rvat, Cappella Giulia, I. 5, f. 43r). In his letter to Martini dated 15 September 1773, Ballabene uses the term 'Mula' when describing his original (but not realised) intent in the *Gloria* 'to set all four subjects of the fugue in Mulas, i. e. cantus firmus' ('avendo io voluto mettere tutti li quattro pensieri della Fuga in Mule, o sia Canto fermo'; I-Bc, Carteggio martiniano, I.030.058).

rhythmic solutions are imposed in order to bypass consecutive intervals at all costs, are quite frequently seen.[6]

The last of these 'exceptions and licences' approved by Martini especially reveal the remarkable price that Ballabene paid in order to accomplish the unprecedented achievement of a real forty-eight-part texture. It is very likely that the resolute critics among his colleagues above all took offence at these aspects: the frequently adventurous melodic shapes in the vocal lines and their intricate and often odd rhythmic features – elements that also would undoubtedly affect the overall aesthetic appearance of the work.

Giuseppe Baini, in his 1828 discourse on the particularities of Palestrina's writing, points out that, in his opinion, the basic problem of polychoral composing (as far as textures for more than twelve real parts are concerned) can be summarised as follows:

> The multiplicity, however, of the twenty, thirty-two, forty, forty-eight parts makes them in the execution, for reasons of common sense and musical philosophy, confused, clamorous, disproportionate, totally devoid of any imitation of nature. . . . Moreover, the highest [manifestation] of the three choirs . . . preserves the true musical beauty in simplicity, clarity, naturalness, golden ease.[7]

This is an undeniable point of criticism of which Ballabene must have been well aware, as his contemporary opponents would have been. But taking into consideration that in his Mass these compositional licences are applied mainly in the tutti sections – and in consideration of the basic inability of the human auditory system to differentiate textures in more than eight real parts – it is of course the eye of the reader (and that of the chorister) rather than the ear of the listener that consciously perceives such exceptions to basic precepts, which thus eventually may only be justified by the end product.

---

6 Foreseeing such harsh concessions, Viadana in 1612 argued firmly in favour of licence-rich writing in polychoral textures: 'And I took a pleasure in doing so, as the music turns out much better; because those who want to compose worthy ripienos have to use rests, quick half-rests, dots, syncopations, which make the music stretched, rustic, and stubborn, always to be sung in a neck-breaking way and with little grace'. ('E così io mi fon compiaciuto di fare, poiche la Mufica riefce affai meglio; percioche chi vuol comporre offeruatamente ne' Ripieni, bifogna feruirfi di paufe, di mezze paufe di fofpiri, di punti, de [sic] fincope, il che fa la Mufica ftiracchiata, ruftica, ed oftinata, cantandofi fempre a rompicollo, e con poca gratia'; Viadana, *Salmi à quattro chori*.)

7 'La molteplicità però delle venti, trentadue, quaranta, quarantotto parti le rende nella esecuzione in ragion di buon senso, e [p. 318] di filosofia musicale confuse, clamorose, di membra sproporzionate, prive totalmente di imitazione della natura. . . . Altronde il sommo dei tre cori . . . conserva il vero bello musicale nella semplicità, chiarezza, naturalezza, aurea facilità'. Baini, *Memorie*, vol. II, p. 317f.

Figure 7.2 Gregorio Ballabene, *Messa a dodici cori*, *Kyrie* I (after I-Rama, A. MS. 316); see also Figure 5.1.

In order to convey an impression of the texture in its complexity, Figure 7.2 gives the first *Kyrie eleison* – 21 bars illustrating several of Ballabene's above-mentioned compositional tools in a very confined space.

Figure 7.2 (Continued)

8 Important compositional features

Despite the public presentation of the *Kyrie* and *Gloria* at Santi XII. Apostoli in 1776, Ballabene's plan to publicly defeat his enemies did not work out. Unfortunately, the hoped-for career jump that the forty-eight-part composition was supposed to guarantee was never achieved, not even in his later years.

Within the framework of this study, the previous consideration of the background and historical circumstances of Ballabene's Mass allows us to gain an idea of the context in which this peculiar work came into existence. A closer look at the technical and artistic qualities will allow a better classification of Ballabene's actual achievement.

First, brief consideration should be given to why the composition does not go beyond the first two movements of the Mass Ordinary: the *Kyrie* and *Gloria*. When he first reached out to Martini on 15 August 1772, Ballabene argued, in a rather flimsy way, that he had concentrated on these two while leaving further movements and especially 'the <u>Creed</u> to a better hand than mine – for ultimate perfection of the Mass'.[1] By covering *Kyrie* I – *Christe* – *Kyrie* II and *Gloria*, Ballabene's work can indeed be considered a 'Mass', albeit in a minimal respect; *Kyrie* or *Gloria* alone could not. One may speculate that *Credo*, *Sanctus*, *Benedictus* and *Agnus Dei* were never intended to be written, owing to the enormous challenge that every single bar of the forty-eight-part texture would have posed for the composer. Furthermore, it may be argued that the traditional practice in polychoral Mass composition by which only a few separate sections within each single movement would have been conceived in a smaller number of parts would have granted little relief to the author. Traditionally, the *Credo* sections such as 'Crucifixus'

---

1 'Avendo voluto lasciare a miglior penna della mia il <u>Credo</u> ad vltimazione perfetta della Meſsa'; I-Bc, Carteggio martiniano, I.030.053. For the quotation in its context see Document 3.

DOI: 10.4324/9781003226710-9

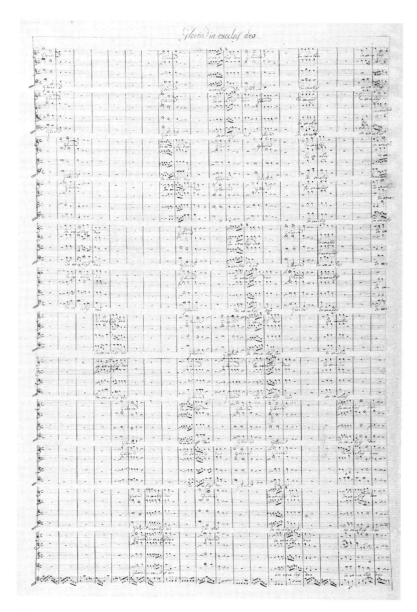

Figure 8.1 Gregorio Ballabene, *Messa a dodici cori*, *Gloria* (beginning), I-Rama, A. MS. 316, f. [4ᵛ].

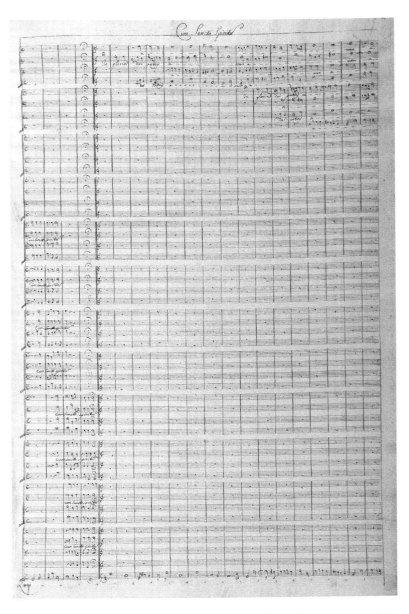

Figure 8.2 Gregorio Ballabene, *Messa a dodici cori*, *Gloria* ('Cum sancto spiritu'), I-Rama, A. MS. 316, f. [9ʳ]: Fugal development in fourfold counterpoint.

Detail ('in gloria Dei patris amen'):
Choirs I and II.

and at times also 'Et resurrexit' and 'Et iterum' were realised by only part of the ensemble (often soloists), likewise the entire *Benedictus* – sections that as a whole would yield only a minor portion of the remaining work.

Another, more important reason for Ballabene's 'self-limitation' to only the *Kyrie* and *Gloria* may be found in the fact that these two movements are sufficient to expose an enormous variety of forty-eight-part contrapuntal structures (the *Christe* is in fact in a real sixteen-part texture, with only four choirs throughout). Had the composer decided to add the other Mass movements, the endeavour would necessarily have required a different overall conception of the work, in an effort to avoid the re-presentation of compositional devices and textures already deployed. As will be seen later, the work in just two movements is indeed conceived according to a thoroughly considered dramaturgy, especially in terms of compositional resources.

As Martini specifies in his approbation, the fundamental quality of the Mass consists of Ballabene's determination not to compromise in basic contrapuntal terms. All forty-eight parts proceed independently from one another; no doubling nor parallel fifths and octaves are tolerated. At the same time, the composer chose to write a remarkably high number of tutti sections, some of which could have been avoided, thereby making the entire enterprise much easier for him as more of the piece could have been realised by less densely woven textures. In this sense, the setting of only *Kyrie* and *Gloria* reflects Ballabene's intention to demonstrate through it his zeal and skilfulness.

Structural and compositional particularities of the work can be summarised as follows:

- Generally speaking, the work deploys textural variety and contrasting combinatory effects, juxtaposing for example twelve-choir tuttis (or smaller-scale settings) with animated sections in which an eight- or sixteen-part texture is passed from one choral group to another, often varying in length and structure, usually in descending order (i.e. from Choir I to Choir XII).[2] Besides the fugue expositions (and not considering the *Christe*), the sounding texture in almost all contexts comprises a minimum of two choirs, often with four choirs singing at a time (very short single-choir sections are the rare exceptions to this rule). In alternating passages, frequently two choirs compete with two others or four with four others. Textures in which the choral tutti alternates with one or two single choruses are not part of Ballabene's conception.

- Apart from polyphonic episodes, the single ensembles generally operate en bloc. Textures in which the intrinsic formation of a choir is exceeded (e.g. when separate parts of several choruses proceed together while the others pause) are completely absent. This feature, often found in works for three to six real choirs (especially by seventeenth-century Roman composers), remains unused by Ballabene in the entire work, even in the sixteen-part *Christe eleison*.

- Notwithstanding such structural premisses, the setting is not dominated by differing combinations of homophonic and homorhythmic passages. Vast fugal textures counterbalance such structures at several prominent points: first, at the opening of *Kyrie* II (where the counterpoint is handed round in a double-choir texture with slightly offset entries, descending from Choir I to Choir XII, before a similar stretto passage prepares the tutti conclusion) and second at the end of the *Gloria* (where, similarly, a fourfold counterpoint is passed from the first choir to the last in consecutive 'waves', dividing the textual passage 'In gloria Dei patris. Amen' in 3 + 2 increasingly narrow 'rounds', each closed by a culminating tutti section). It goes without saying that in a performance in which the twelve ensembles are spatially dislocated, such sectionwise 'wandering sound plains' will generate stunning effects for the listener.

- The phenomenon called 'Mula', the doubling in unison of an entire vocal register across all choruses (in the present case, all the sopranos) in long values and over large sections, is used towards the end of *Kyrie* II and in the final 'Amen' of the *Gloria* (for the closing part of the *Gloria*, the

---

2 See Figure 8.1 or Figure 7.2 (bars 5–8). The concept of 'descent' here refers to the visual disposition of the choirs in the score, with Choir I at the top and Choir XII at the bottom.

soprano Mula is even accompanied by a separate Mula line in the unified altos, like a two-part cantus firmus, first in binary and then in ternary metre). In both movements, this particular artifice provokes a marked increase in textural intensity, in addition to the amplification of the parts concerned, thus lending additional strength to the effect of final closure.

It has been noticed earlier in connection with Martini's *Descrizione* – and here especially in the instance of Pitoni's attempt to compose a similar work – that a forty-eight-part contrapuntal texture as the basic feature of a musical setting has far-reaching consequences for the arrangement in general. This particularly applies to rhythm, voice-leading and harmonic progression. Apart from these conditions, an economy of musical means can also be observed in Ballabene's work, cleverly arranged to develop every single movement or section with increasing intensity. Including this aspect in a critical reading of the work, Martini's high regard, witnessed throughout his *Descrizione*, albeit with restraint, can hardly be countered with rational arguments.

The essential individuality of this multivoiced setting results from the observance of contrapuntal necessities on the one hand and far-reaching structural decisions on the other, most evident in the tutti textures. These basic elements are characterised in particular by the following compositional-technical properties:

- *Peculiar rhythms in almost all parts*
  Application of this device is not necessarily in pursuance of rhythmic complementarity of textures; rather, it is a compelling consequence of the requirement to avoid parallels in voice-leading. The compromising nature of this feature is clear (especially in the rhythmically 'staggered' progressions set in order to avoid unisons, fifths or octaves through slightly displacing the relevant melodic motion or by inserting short rests), as the resulting aural impression does not always turn out satisfactorily – unless the device is covered up by the density of the surrounding tutti texture.

- *Odd melodic writing, especially in middle voices*
  In sustained harmonies – but notably in changing harmonies – the composer is compelled to introduce voice-leading that tolerates the most unusual interval steps, such as sevenths, which frequently appear in cadences (e.g. as a downward leap from the leading note to the final resolution or from the fifth of the dominant to the third of the tonic). And in order to avoid doubling, unprepared and even irregularly resolved dissonances are encountered, which in a single vocal line can lead to convoluted twists.

- *Slow harmonic rhythm*
  Whatever applies to polychoral textures in general applies even more to a twelve-choir setting: in a dense polyphonic structure, especially with regard to parallels, changing harmonies are more difficult to handle than sustained harmonies. Consequently, harmonic progressions (especially in tutti sections) often move slowly, in binary metre and seldom faster than in semibreves.

- *Nonobservance of the bass rule*
  In common seventeenth- and eighteenth-century polychoral composition, the bottom line of every chorus is by definition the harmonic reference point for the remaining parts. In Ballabene's setting this 'bass rule' is relaxed: the vocal bass parts do not proceed in unison, but they often do not even coincide with the continuo line, as the functional fundamental part of their chorus. As a consequence, the fifth in the bass part frequently causes 6/4 chords, the seventh 6/4/2 chords and so on, circumstances that are 'recovered' in harmonic terms only by the fundamental basso continuo line, a virtually indispensable element of all the choruses. With the suspension of the bass rule, the composer, who a priori conceived the organ part as a traditional *basso seguente*, gains additional margin in regard to voice-leading. The use of this licence is, however, limited principally to the tutti sections.

- *Single-register 'Mula' as a tool for boosting intensity*
  The section 'In gloria Dei patris. Amen' at the end of the *Gloria* (which as part of Ballabene's dramaturgical scheme opens towards the triumphant conclusion of the work as a whole) is conceived as a fugal texture with four subjects in binary metre, divided into several developments of growing intensity, in terms of compositional devices (Figure 8.2, 8.3a–c). In the first development, only two or three choirs perform at a time (beginning with Choir I, in descending order and with ever shorter entries, down to Choir XII). The end of the section is overlapped by a second stretto-like development, opening with Choir I again, but this time its entry flows into a Mula that unifies the sopranos of all twelve choirs. Simultaneously, the fugal development continues, now in the intensified form of three to four choirs at a time, in the same order, before a short section forms the tutti: now even the twelve alto parts unify in a nine-bar-long Mula, the period concludes with a cadence and the metre comes to a halt on a fermata.

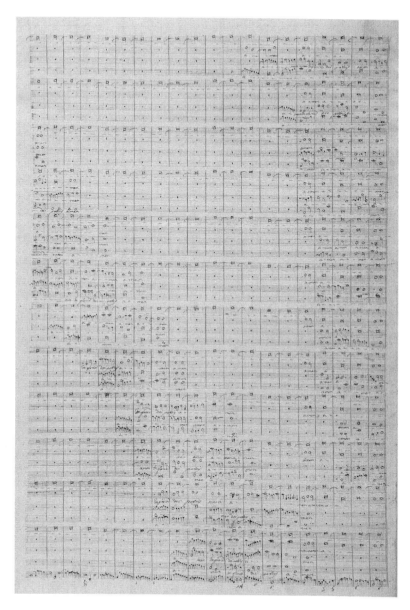

Figure 8.3a Gregorio Ballabene, *Messa a dodici cori*, *Gloria* ('Cum sancto spiritu'), I-Rama, A. MS. 316, f. [10ᵛ]: Two-part Mula in binary metre.

Detail ('in gloria Dei patris amen'):
Choirs I–III.

• *Double-register 'Mula' for an additional increase towards the crowning conclusion*

What follows now is a further intensification of the spirit of the movement. The final 'Amen' is set in ternary metre (3/2). The relatively swift choral development establishes a double-choir texture, in which a short section of two to three bars' length is handed round, descending from Choirs I and II down to Choirs XI and XII. In a second, more rapid, development a similar order is followed, but before Choirs XI and XII round off, the united tutti enters powerfully for the concluding section. Now another, longer double-register Mula is established, again between sopranos and altos, containing a seven-bar sequence of dissonances (7–6). Immediately afterwards, the altos return to independent lines, whereas the sopranos stay unified for the remaining seven bars, sustaining the final note like a pedal point radiating above the plagal-cadencing tutti closure (Figure 8.3c).[3]

3 Among the known cases in seventeenth- and eighteenth-century Roman polychoral repertoire where this compositional device is applied, the final section of Ballabene's *Gloria* is the only one that features a double-register 'Mula'. This innovative feature may be considered as *pars pro toto* for Ballabene's autonomy regarding the technical and stylistic advancement of the genre.

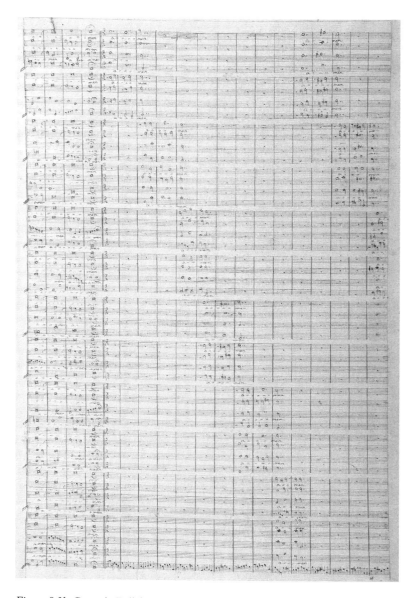

Figure 8.3b Gregorio Ballabene, *Messa a dodici cori*, *Gloria* ('Cum sancto spiritu'), I-Rama, A. MS. 316, f. [11ʳ]: End of two-part Mula in binary metre and beginning of development in ternary metre.

Detail:
Choirs I–IV.

It should be added that the construction of *Kyrie* II demonstrates a dramaturgical conception analogous to that of the *Gloria*, although on a smaller
scale, thus giving the sequence of *Kyrie* I-*Christe*-*Kyrie* II an intrinsically
contrasting character. With that in mind, the structure of Ballabene's work
as a whole can be considered an intriguing manifestation of 'musical archi-
tecture' – an overall impression confirmed on closer inspection.

At first sight, Ballabene's monumental opus may impress through its
technical complexity, and it is understandable that the first thing Otto
Nicolai (1810–1849) noticed in 1835 during his stay in Rome was that
'human combinatory powers have probably not yet gone any further'.[4]

4 'Ballabene Kyrie e Gloria a 48 (weiter ist wohl menschliches Combinationsvermögen noch
   nicht gegangen)'. Nicolai (Rome) in his letter to Georg Poelchau (Berlin) dated 20 September 1835; reproduced in Vierneisel, 'Otto Nicolai', p. 234. For Nicolai's role regarding the
   transmission of the manuscript, see Chapter 12, The history of the score.

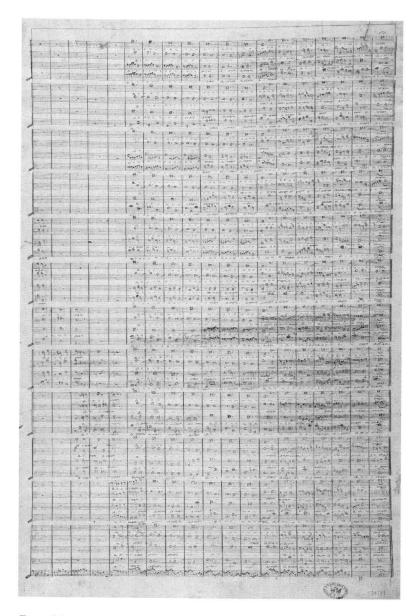

Figure 8.3c Gregorio Ballabene, *Messa a dodici cori, Gloria* ('Cum sancto spiritu'), I-Rama, A. MS. 316, f. [11ᵛ]: Two-part Mula in ternary metre and conclusion.

Detail ('amen'):
Choirs I–IV.

Yet, close up, the Mass turns out to be more than an encyclopaedic treatise of polyphonic progressions designed to illustrate all the imaginable
compositional challenges that could ever be posed by a dense contrapuntal
structure in real parts. More than being a refined object of study and theoretical demonstration, it is sensational from an aesthetic point of view – it not
only proves the practicability of a real forty-eight-part texture but also lays
claim to being a thoroughly sophisticated work of art. Moreover, aspects
of the work can even be said to be relevant to intellectual history, as will
be explained.

The challenge of conceiving two mass movements 'a 48' has been successfully met, whereas any functional use of Ballabene's work remains
hardly imaginable – especially in a liturgical context – and for all sorts of

reasons. It remains the case nonetheless that all document-based observations need to be put to the test by a diligently prepared modern-day performance. The work is unlikely ever to become part of the concert repertoire, but exposure to a practical rendition is ultimately needed in order for the qualities (and defects) of the work to be properly revealed.

9 Pitoni's Mass

As already mentioned, Giuseppe Ottavio Pitoni (1657–1743) was the only other composer in Roman music history to attempt to write a Mass for twelve real choirs. The score is missing, and one of the most trustworthy documents regarding the work is a biographical sketch drawn by Pitoni's former student Girolamo Chiti (1679–1759) in 1744. In this posthumous homage, Chiti affirms:

> Among his other works, he [Pitoni] began a Mass for twelve choruses, i. e. for forty-eight real voices, in which he wrote down the twelve bass and the twelve soprano parts, and filled in all forty-eight parts of the first Kyrie and the Christe. But he could not finish it, asserting on many an occasion that it would take two years at least to complete. Spending at least two hours a day of serious effort on it, and being of a very advanced age, he was not able to finish that laborious task, so this Mass remained incomplete and is kept at the music archive of the Vatican.[1]

According to this note, Pitoni (who had been *maestro di cappella* at St Peter's since 1719 until his death) took on the challenge only very late in his career,

---

1 '[Pitoni] principiò frà l'altre Sue Opere Vna Mefsa a Dodici Cori, cioe a quaranta otto Voci reali, nella quale Intauolo tutte le parti de dodici Bafsi e dodici Soprani, e riempi ancora tutte le quaranta e otto parti del p.ᵐᵒ Chijrie e del Christe, ne la pote Terminare[,] afserendo piu uolte che p. Compirla ci Voleuano almeno Sopra due anni col farci pero serio Studio almeno due ora [sic] ogni giorno, et efsendo il medefimo auanzato in età graue[,] non poteua ultimare tal fatigofo Impegno, la qual Mefsa e reftata Imperfetta e sta nell'Archiuio Muficale del Vaticano'. Girolamo Chiti, 'Riftretto della Vita, et opere del m.ᵗᵒ eccell.ᵗᵉ Sig.ʳ Giuseppe Ottauio Pitoni Romano, Maeftro di Cappella della Sacro Santa Bafilica di S. Pietro in Vaticano e della Cappella Giulia', MS, dated 'Roma li 23 Luglio 1744', I-Rvat, Cappella Giulia, III. 56, f. [5r/v]; a modern edition of the document is included in Pitoni, *Notitia*, pp. 351–356.

DOI: 10.4324/9781003226710-10

apparently around 1740, almost as if it were an attempt finally to realise a project to which he had long aspired. Pitoni wrote more than 3,000 sacred works, among them 247 Masses. Besides his official duties and obligations, he dedicated a lifetime to the creation of a gargantuan encyclopaedia of harmonic progressions entitled *Guida armonica*.[2] In light of this enterprise, it seems that he may have contemplated the practical challenge of composing for forty-eight real parts as the ideal culmination of such a theoretical magnum opus. However, like the *Guida armonica*, the Mass remained unfinished: as Chiti mentions, only *Kyrie* I and the *Christe* were completed.

Chiti was *maestro di cappella* at the Lateran from 1727 onwards. In his later years he was the principal Roman correspondent of Padre Martini,[3] and it is most likely due to this vivid exchange that Pitoni's Mass project was brought to the latter's attention. The occasion on which Chiti shared with Martini his biographical notes on Pitoni (presumably during the later 1740s) may be considered the *terminus post quem* for Martini's knowledge of the twelve-choir Mass. Surprisingly, however, specific references to the work are lacking in their extant correspondence.

In 1753, during a visit to Rome, Martini obtained permission to consult the Pitoni manuscript, which together with Pitoni's other sacred works had been transferred to the Vatican after his death. Giovanni Biordi, dean of the papal chapel, showed him the incomplete score, which Martini considered 'a sketch'.[4] This impression seems to reflect the composition process Chiti

---

2   The *Guida armonica* was conceived to illustrate analytically all possible interval progressions between two parts. Pitoni had commenced working on it long before the 1700s, and although it was brought to an advanced state, it remained incomplete. At his death in 1743 only one volume had been printed. The 22 volumes of material, plus another 19 bundles of drafts, templates and revisions, which in total amount to more than 30,000 sheets of text, are housed in I-Rvat, Cappella Giulia, I/4–44. Concerning the colossal undertaking see Grampp, '. . . Benche i maestri'.

3   Their correspondence in I-Bc, covering the relatively short period 1745–1759, counts 438 letters; see Rostirolla et al., *Epistolario*, and Rostirolla, 'La corrispondenza'. For Martini's manuscript copy of Chiti's 'Vita di Giuseppe Ottavio Pitoni', see I-Bc, G.6 (Olim Cod. 075:11).

4   'Un'abbozzo di una Meſſa conſimile a 48. voci, che favorì farmi vedere nell'anno 1753. il degniſſimo Signor Gio: Biordi allora Decano de' Cantori Pontifizj'; Martini, *Descrizione*, p. XI (see Document 4). In 1753 Martini had come to Rome to direct the festive music during the Triduum scheduled at Santi XII. Apostoli on occasion of the beatification of Giuseppe da Copertino, OFM Conv. The official recognition of the Blessed had been accorded on 24 February; the festivities of the order followed on 18–20 September (*Diario ordinario*, no. 5646, 22 September 1753, pp. 7–8). Martini directed the music for two Masses and three Vespers, each with different music ('nei d.ⁱ tre giorni [il d.° P. Martini] fece tanto le due Messe, come li 3 Vesperi sempre differenti'), as reported by Pier Leone Ghezzi,

had outlined, according to which Pitoni first composed the outer parts of all choruses, before subsequently inserting the middle parts.

Another important aspect came to Martini's attention two decades later, as he set down his *Descrizione* in 1774. Recalling the impact that the inspection of Pitoni's score had had on him, he points out: 'Pitoni, however, was not committed (as also in his four-choir compositions) to real diversity of the 48 parts. Instead, he allowed several of them to sing in unison, now with these, now with those parts of the other choirs'.[5] This observation is important as it makes clear that what Martini witnessed in 1753 and what Ballabene presented to him in 1772 were two different works. The presence of only *Kyrie* I and the *Christe* in Pitoni's 'sketch' is another feature that distinguishes it from Ballabene's setting. The latter, in terms of structure and extent, is necessarily more comprehensive than the former, if only owing to the musical challenges the amount of extra text would have imposed on the author.

The fact that Pitoni's Mass 'sketch' is lost may initially raise suspicions concerning Ballabene's authorship of the work he ambitiously tried to promote in the 1770s.[6] Such presumption, however, can be rebutted by the details about Pitoni's work that emerge from Chiti's and Martini's discussions, which are clearly incompatible with the features exhibited by Ballabene's composition. It is to be hoped that Pitoni's manuscript, supposedly a bulky volume with dimensions analogous to those of the extant sources of the Ballabene Mass (see Appendix II), may still re-emerge, thus enabling a comparison of Ballabene's work with the only approximately similar composition.

who even left a drawing of Martini's musical direction (reproduced in Rostirolla et al., *Il 'Mondo novo'*, illustration no. 375).

It might be added here that in Rome and well into the nineteenth century, it was by no means easy to gain access to important music collections; guardians of private or ecclesiastical archives tended to be dismissive and reserved rather than complaisant and helpful. The fact that gates were opened for interested visitors such as Martini or Burney and later Fortunato Santini must be seen as the result of diplomatic efforts and networking, made possible through recommendations and gifts or articles of exchange and often due to highly individual circumstances. For the corresponding situation in Santini's years see Rostirolla, 'Riletture', p. 337.

5   'Non volle però il Pitoni obbligarfi (ficcome fece anche nelle fue compofizioni a 4. Cori) alla reale diverfità delle 48. Parti; ma fece, che varie di effe cantaffero in uniffono, ora con alcune, ora con altre Parti degli altri Cori'; Martini, *Descrizione*, p. XIf.

6   It is unclear when Pitoni's composition disappeared. In Lichtenthal's dictionary (1836), both the Pitoni and the Ballabene Mass are still mentioned as legendary examples of twelve-choir writing, but anything more specific than that is already missing at that point ('vi sono de' pezzi di musica persino di *dodici Cori reali*, come di Ballabene, di Pittoni'; Lichtenthal, 'Coro reale').

10 Ballabene and the twilight of an era

Apart from Ballabene's institutional role from the 1780s onwards as one of the examiners of the *maestri di cappella* section of the Congregazione di Santa Cecilia, there is no evidence of any greater career successes after the 1776 Mass rehearsal. In fact, it seems that up to this point powerful adversaries within the congregation itself had hindered any advancement.[1] Despite all Ballabene's endeavours, any effect of the Mass rehearsal on his professional career was very modest: still in the 1780s, he continued to find himself compelled to teach children at an orphanage in order to make a living.[2]

In a sacred libretto printed in Gubbio in 1784, the composer of the music, Ballabene, is designated as 'illustrious *maestro di cappella* at Rome' yet without specifying where he held the post, as would have been customary.[3] Evidently there was still no prestigious title with which the composer could adorn himself. In the same year, Padre Martini (Bologna) once more advocates for Ballabene, this time in a letter to Sabbatini (dated 21 July):

> Mr Ballabene, a famous man who . . . accomplished the great work of a
> Mass for 48 voices, a work the likes of which had never been seen in the

---

1 Giovanni Battista Costanzi (1704–1778), *maestro* of the Cappella Giulia at St Peter's and Antonio Aurisicchio (1710–1781), a powerful figure within the congregation until 1780, were apparently the most prominent and influential among Ballabene's critics. According to a letter by Ballabene's *maestro di cappella* colleague Giambattista Casali to Martini, dated 27 December 1775, both Aurisicchio and Costanzi, whom Casali openly calls fools ('due Sciocchi de nostri'), had only recently confirmed their opposition to the forty-eight-part Mass, declaring it impracticable ('che non era eseguibile'). In this context, Ballabene had asked Casali, as previously he had asked Martini, for a written approval regarding his Mass, which Casali promised to issue (I-Bc, Carteggio martiniano, I.021.036).
2 See Chapter 12, n. 13.
3 'Mufica del sig. Gregorio Ballabene celebre maeftro di cappella in Roma'; Ceccarelli, *Poesia per musica*, p. [4]; printed libretto in I-Vgc, ROLANDI ROL.0149.25.

DOI: 10.4324/9781003226710-11

past, and which has been ridiculed by his colleagues, but which, upon the order of the lately deceased Most Eminent Cardinal Albani, was defended by me, who also described the value and merit of the author.[4]

Here Martini incidentally admits that the public defence of the work in the 1770s – a decade earlier – had taken place at the behest of the cardinal, information that supposedly had been kept under wraps as long as the powerful clergyman was alive. Nonetheless, it is evident that Martini still fully stands by his word and his decision to support Ballabene's cause.

And yet, all this goodwill did not help the Roman master gain a more honourable position.[5] After Martini's death in 1784, Ballabene tried to initiate a correspondence with Martini's assistant and successor, Father Stanislao Mattei OFM Conv (1750–1825), but this exchange also seems not to have had any far-reaching consequences.[6] In biographical terms, no further career highlights are known. Ballabene seems to have died between 1800 and 1803, possibly not in Rome, as neither a death record nor a will has been traced in Roman archives.

The twelve-choir Mass is not the only polychoral composition among Ballabene's *oeuvre*. A *Magnificat a 16* in four choirs, dated 1778, exists in autograph score, and although a sixteen-part *Dixit Dominus* (1796) and a *Dixit Dominus a 4 cori con l'intonazione sesto tuono* with orchestral accompaniment (1782) are mentioned in literature, all traces of them are lost.[7]

---

4 'Il Sig. Ballabene, uomo celebre, il quale . . . fece la grand'opera della Meſsa a 48. Voci, Opera che per il paſsato non si è mai veduta, e che fù poſta in ridicolo dai suoi Colleghi, ma che per comando dell'E.mo Sig. Cardinale Albani ultimo deffunto fù da me difeſa, e ne fù deſcritto il valore e il merito dell'autore'; I-Bc, Carteggio martiniano, I.029.007a.

5 In the ranks of the Roman confraternity of musicians, only posthumously (in 1845) is his name given among the 'masters who distinguished themselves within our congregation from the beginning of the eighteenth century until present' ('maestri che si distinsero nella nostra Congregazione dal principio del secolo decimo ottavo fino al presente'; Alfieri, *Brevi notizie*, p. 22).

6 The two extant letters from Ballabene in Rome to Mattei in Bologna mainly revolve around his condolences on Martini's death (letter dated 27 October 1784; I-Bsf, MS 60, no. 13) and his attempt to promote Catalisano's 1781 book *Grammatica-armonica* (see Chapter 6, n. 12), in which Ballabene himself is mentioned (letter dated 4 December 1784; I-Bsf, MS 60, no. 14). Ballabene's proposal in that matter may have been successful, as today the Catalisano volume is still part of the convent library (I-Bc, F. 90). Martini, however, had known about the work even before it had been printed, as his correspondence with Catalisano from autumn 1780 shows (see in particular I-Bc, Carteggio martiniano, L.117.040 and 040a).

7 The *Magnificat a 16* (1778) is kept in GB-Lcm, RCM MS 748. In 1910, a 'Magnificat a 16 (1778)', a 'Dixit Dominus a 16 (1796)' and a 'Dixit Dominus a 4 cori con l'intonazione sesto tono con Violini, Oboè, Trombe, Corni, Viole ed Organo' by Ballabene were still mentioned as elements of the Santini collection (Killing, *Kirchenmusikalische Schätze*,

It may be added that next to Pisari and Ballabene some other late representatives of the 'Roman school' are known to have sporadically composed polychoral works, among them Giovanni Battista Costanzi (1704–1778), director of the Cappella Giulia and famous for a *Dixit Dominus* for four choirs, and Sante Pesci (ca 1712–1786), renowned *maestro di cappella* and author of a sixteen-part Mass.[8] Another papal singer, Giovanni Battista Fazzini (fl. 1774–1799), left a *Dixit a sedici voci*, in four choirs with instruments, dedicated to Cardinal Giovanni Battista Rezzonico in 1780.[9] Giuseppe Jannacconi (1741–1816) is the author of (among other works) a sixteen-part *Te Deum* in four choirs (dated 1800), a sixteen-part *Kyrie* and a sixteen-part *Magnificat*,[10] whereas his prominent scholar Baini left no works for more than two choirs.

p. 475). A four-choir *Dixit* by Ballabene, dated 1782, was still listed in Fellerer's 1929 exhibition catalogue as part of the collection (Fellerer, *Die musikalischen Schätze*, p. 16). The work-lists in several later music dictionaries (e.g. *Dizionario enciclopedico universale della musica e dei musicisti*, *The New Grove Dictionary of Music and Musicians*, *Die Musik in Geschichte und Gegenwart*) are based on Killing's and Fellerer's registers.

8 The main source for this information is Baini, writing in 1808: 'Giovanni Costanzi . . . Maestro of the Cappella Giulia at the Vatican Basilica collected for years the praises of all Rome with a most excellent <u>Dixit</u> for <u>four choruses</u> performed repeatedly in Santa Maria in Aracoeli [the church of the Roman Senate] for the feast of St Rose of Viterbo' ('Giovanni Costanzi . . . Maestro della Cappella Giulia nella Basilica Vaticana si procacciò per diversi anni gli encomj di tutta Roma con eccellentissimo <u>Dixit</u> a <u>Quattro Cori</u> eseguito ripetutamente in S. Maria in Ara Caeli per la festa di S. Rosa da Viterbo'; Baini, 'Mottetto', p. 5). The score of a four-choir *Dixit Dominus* by Costanzi (dated 1746) is extant in D-MÜs (SANT Hs 1299). On Pesci, Baini states that 'Sante Pesci, chapel master at the Liberian Basilica [i.e. Santa Maria Maggiore], who died around 1790, received the applause of the entire profession for a sixteen-part Mass performed in the church of San Carlo ai Catinari [the church of the Congregazione di Santa Cecilia] for St Cecilia's Day' ('Sante Pesci Maestro della Basilica Liberiana morto circa il 1790. ricevette gli applausi di tutta la professione per una Messa a Sedici Voci eseguita in S. Carlo a' Catinari per la festa di S. Cecilia'; Baini, 'Mottetto', p. 5). For an early nineteenth-century copy of an analogous work by Pesci see D-MÜs, SANT Hs 3145.

9 D-MÜs, SANT Hs 1492.

10 Parts and score of the Jannacconi *Te Deum* are in I-Rsg, B. 991 and 992. According to a note in the score, the work was written at the election of Pope Pius VII (elected 14 March 1800) in Venice and performed again at another festive event in 1820 in Ancona. Jannacconi was a tenor of the Cappella Giulia at St Peter's. His candidacies for important *maestro di cappella* positions (at Milan Cathedral in 1779 and at the Cappella Giulia in 1793 and 1805) were unsuccessful. His *Kyrie* (deriving from his Milan candidacy, see I-Mfd, A. D., Busta 22, no. 1, int. 2454; copy in D-MÜs, SANT Hs xy 301) cannot be classified as polychoral, being conceived as 'Fuga a 16. voci all'Organo tirata a Canone perpetuo' (according to the source in I-Mfd, the work was already written in 1767). Among Jannacconi's polychoral works in the Santini collection, only the four-choir motet 'Tu es Petrus a 16 con org', according to Killing dated 1802, is still extant (D-MÜs, SANT Hs 2177),

From outside the Roman school there is Marco Santucci (1762–1843), a student of Fedele Fenaroli in Naples who in 1797 briefly served as *maestro di cappella* at the Lateran. The only known polychoral work of his is a motet for sixteen parts in four choirs, *Sancta Cecilia ora pro nobis*, written as early as 1780.[11] With this composition, described as a 'work of a new kind' ('lavoro di genere nuovo') in 1806, Santucci even won the newly established music prize of the Accademia Napoleone in Lucca. As a consequence, the work was published the same year.[12] Despite such a spectacular success, the setting proves to be texturally of only moderate quality and was considered insignificant by contemporaneous experts aware of the historical background of the genre. In his publication *Lettera sopra il mottetto a quattro cori del sig. D. Marco Santucci premiato dall'accademia Napoleone in Lucca l'anno 1806. come lavoro di genere nuovo*, Baini heavily criticised the work in relation to prominent exponents of the art, such as Agostini, Benevoli, Abbatini or Berretta. Ironising the prize-winning work, he argues that in view of a century-long tradition of polychoral composing in which works for twenty, twenty-four, thirty-two and even forty-eight parts in twelve choruses (!) had been masterfully conceived, a four-choir composition could hardly represent an innovation of any kind, and furthermore, he accuses Santucci of having been aware of this larger background.[13]

whereas the following works are missing: 'Dixit Dominus . . . a 16 c[on] b[asso] c[ontinuo] in quinto tono', 'Magnificat a 16 con org. e contrabasso (1804)' and 'Messa concert[ata] a 16 solenne con org' (Killing, *Kirchenmusikalische Schätze*, pp. 498–499). The works (including the *Te Deum*) are still part of Fellerer's catalogue (Fellerer, 'Verzeichnis': 30 (1935), pp. 152–155) but are missing in Wörmann's (Wörmann, [Catalogue]). The sixteen-part 'M[iss]a solenne', dated 1802, is furthermore registered in Hüntemann, *Die Messen*, p. 24. A largely similar account is given in Kindler, 'Verzeichnis'. Jannacconi's four-choir *Te Deum* (I-Rsg, B. 991 and 992) is not included in the catalogue of his works proposed in Kantner, '*Aurea Luce*', pp. 306–308).

11 Manuscript copies in D-B (score and parts, Mus.MS 19430 and 19430/1), I-Ria (MSS Vess. 263) and A-Ed (B 289).

12 *Mottetto Sancta Cecilia ora pro nobis a Quattro Cori Reali. A S. A. Imperiale e Reale la Principessa Elisa, composizione coronata del Sig. Maestro di Cappella D. Marco Santucci* (Lucca: F. Bertini, 1806; RISM SS 904 I,4). The official justification for the acknowledgement is given in *Atti della solenne adunanza*, pp. 21–23 (see Document 15b).

13 A copy of Baini's print is presently untraceable. In his *Memorie* (Baini, *Memorie*, vol. II, p. 316, n. 636), he provides the title given here. The previous paraphrase of the content of his *Lettera* is based on a biographical sketch published in 1845, the year after Baini's death, in the *Gazzetta musicale di Milano* (de la Fage, 'Studj Biografici'). As part of Baini's estate there is an autograph version of the *Lettera* entitled 'Mottetto a Quattro Cori del Sig.ʳ Maestro D. Marco Santucci premiato dall'Accademia Napoleone in Lucca l'anno 1806. Esaminato e Criticato da Giufeppe Baini Cappellano Cantore Pontificio', dated 1808 (I-Rc, MS 2895). In a total of eighty-seven pages, Baini not only scrutinises the winning composition and comments on the commission's judgement but also presents a detailed historical

In fact, Santucci's poorly crafted sixteen-part setting is full of octave leaps and broken-chord melodies in all parts, while on the twenty-one pages (118 bars) of the score not a single contrapuntal development worthy of the name can be found. In addition, the vocal lines are largely unsingable for a texture of only sixteen parts.

In later years, Gaetano Gaspari (1807–1881), librarian of the Liceo Musicale di Bologna, published a truly devastating comment on 'this miserable composition' ('questa meschina composizione') in his catalogue of the library holdings, asking in conclusion: 'How could highly renowned maestri

essay on polychorality in practice and in theory in which, by means of comprehensive contextualisation, he highlights the fact that Santucci's work cannot by any means be placed within the history of the genre. Regarding textures for forty-eight parts, Baini already knew about Ballabene's Mass when writing his *Lettera* in 1807/1808, as he quotes at length both from Martini's *Descrizione* (1774) and from his *Saggio fondamentale* (1774–1775), where Ballabene is briefly mentioned (see Baini, 'Mottetto', pp. 11, 16–18, 42). Among Baini's papers there is even an undated partial score of the Mass, copied by himself (Appendix II, no. 14). Baini must have held the work in the highest regard, as according to his autograph notes in his copy it is considered 'A truly golden work', 'A work worthy of veneration' ('Opus vere aureum', 'Opus cedro dignissimum').

Nonetheless Baini refrained from articulating any other public statement about Ballabene and his masterpiece. One can only speculate whether when he was writing his *Memorie* in the 1820s, Ballabene's historical reputation was still characterised by the 1776 experience, so that Baini could not extol the qualities of the Mass (unless, of course, he in fact obtained his own copy at a much later date). In 1828, however, when referring to Martini's *Descrizione* (1774), Baini limits what he says to a description of its contents, according to which Martini 'detects the fine harmonic beauties of such a daring composition, supported by twelve different basses simultaneously' ('rileva le fine bellezze armoniche di così azzardata composizione, retta da dodici bassi diversi, e simultanei'; Baini, *Memorie*, vol. II, p. 364). However, in his 1808 comment on Santucci's motet, he had already expressed appreciation for Ballabene's sixteen-part *Christe eleison* (a section not comprised in his partial copy of the score), with information that is contained neither in Martini's *Descrizione* (1774) nor in his *Saggio fondamentale* (1774–1775): 'Ballabene . . . set the <u>Christe</u> for 16 concerted parts, in response to those who might bemoan that after a full 48 parts it would need a lesser number for the listeners to hear it with delight' ('Ballabene . . . fece il <u>Christe</u> concertato a 16., rispondendo a chi se ne maravigliava, che dopo un pieno di 48. voci non vi voleva di manco perchè gli Uditori l'ascoltassero con gusto'; Baini, 'Mottetto', p. 42).

Having mentioned Ballabene's Mass in his *Memorie* in a rather reserved tone (and literally reduced to a footnote), Baini played an important role in the reception history of the work, especially due to the 1834 German edition of the study (Kandler – Kiesewetter, *Ueber das Leben*). It will remain unknown to what extent Baini's uncle Lorenzo (1740–1814), former *maestro di cappella* at Santi XII. Apostoli and presumably a witness to the 1776 rehearsal, influenced his nephew's attitude towards and knowledge about the Mass.

express so ridiculous a vote, to put it mildly, and be altogether so overly poor of expertise not to discern good from bad in terms of musical composition'.[14]

In context, the previously mentioned (mostly solitary) compositions by Pisari and Ballabene, Costanzi and Pesci, Fazzini and Jannacconi cannot really be considered testimonies of a vibrant Roman polychoral sacred-music culture in the proper sense. Rather they take the appearance of 'monuments', commemorating the heyday of the genre: antiquated manifestations of an epic musical past.[15] The to-some-extent metaphorical case of the Santucci motet demonstrates that by the turn of the nineteenth century polychorality, even in rather illustrious circles of sacred music, had fallen into oblivion to such an extent that even in its homeland a four-choir work of minor value would be passed off as a great novelty.[16] And it is with this bizarre episode that the era of one of the most intriguing musical phenomena, Roman polychoral sacred music, finally came to an end.

14 'Come potessero maestri di grido emettere un voto così ridicolo per non dir altro, e fossero insieme cotanto poveri di scienza da non discernere il buono dal cattivo in fatto di musicali componimenti'; Gaspari, *Catalogo*, vol. I, p. 95. For the quotation in its context see Document 15a. In the judges' justification for presenting the prize to Santucci in 1806, the names of the music commission members of the Accademia Napoleone are not indicated (*Atti della solenne adunanza*, pp. 21–23). The reasoning set out by the commission is reproduced in Document 15b.

15 Concerning Jannacconi and also Ballabene, this seems only partially true, in light of their lifelong (yet not very successful) attempts to continue the tradition of polychoral composition, as reflected by the relatively large number of their documented works for four choirs.

16 In this context it must be added that Lucca's Accademia Napoleone was an honourable humanist institution dedicated to the support of science and scholarship, refounded under its new name in 1805. In that year the small Republic of Lucca had become 'Principality of Lucca and Piombino' for the will of Napoleon Bonaparte, who installed his sister Elisa (1777–1820) as ruling princess. Even though the academy enjoyed an Italy-wide reputation, the experts responsible for awarding the prize to Santucci were clearly subjected to the will of Santucci's patroness, whose enduring protection he enjoyed. (The score of his motet is, of course, dedicated to the princess: 'A S[ua] A[ltezza] Imperiale e Reale | La Principessa Elisa'.) Santucci furthermore became canon at Lucca Cathedral (1808) and was also member of the music section of the academy. He spent the rest of his career in Lucca, where he died in 1843.

11 Fame and posthumous fame

After the 1776 rehearsal there is no evidence of any further exchange between Ballabene and Martini. Ballabene's name does not appear in Martini's *Storia della musica* (published in three volumes between 1757 and 1781), which focuses on ancient music. On the other hand, the composer is explicitly praised in Martini's counterpoint treatise *Saggio fondamentale pratico di contrapunto sopra il canto fermo*, which was published in two volumes in 1774–1775, just after the *Descrizione* had been printed. In the entire work, however, Ballabene is mentioned only once: when talking about the suspension of leading notes in polychoral textures and about ways to resolve them correctly without causing parallels. Here Martini extols the artifices that in such contexts have been demonstrated exemplarily by Benevoli in his works 'and in our days laudably by Gregorio Ballabene in his most elaborate composition of *Kyrie* and *Gloria in excelsis* for forty-eight voices distributed in twelve choirs'.[1] Behind this succinct statement one may cautiously surmise a certain uneasiness on Martini's part, and the fact that Ballabene's giant contrapuntal construct is not mentioned again in the entire 600-page *Saggio* might indicate that Martini had some less-than-positive associations with the author and his work.

After the publication of Martini's *Descrizione*, scholarly interest was awakened – not so much in the composer but rather in his henceforth famed Mass. In December 1774 the Bolognese organist Pietro Morandi (1745–1815) contacted Martini to enquire if it was true that Ballabene wrote 'a Mass for 24 [sic] Choirs . . . because it seems impossible to me that this

---

1 'Queſto è uno di quei ſingolari Artificj uſati dalla Scuola Romana del Secolo paſſato, e praticato ſingolarmente nelle Compoſizioni a 2. 3. 4. e più Cori da Orazio Benevoli, e a' giorni noſtri lodevolmente da Gregorio Ballabene nella ſua laborioſiſſima Compoſizione dei *Kyrie*, e *Gloria in excelſis* a quarantotto Voci diſtribuite in dodici Cori'; Martini, *Saggio*, vol. II (1775), p. 279.

DOI: 10.4324/9781003226710-12

man knows how to shape counterpoint of this kind'. He asks for confirmation that Martini himself approved the work – as, if this is the case, he would like to own a copy of the score.[2] It seems that Ballabene's reputation as a composer and the achievement his work represented (even, according to rumours, with twenty-four choirs instead of twelve) were not on a par with one another. As early as April that year, Martini had already received a similar request from another highly incredulous colleague.[3]

In April 1775 the French journal *L'esprit des journaux*, a monthly published digest of the international press, proffered a detailed description of Ballabene's work, which on closer inspection turns out to be largely a translation of Martini's *Descrizione*, without much independent content. The article is the only known contemporaneous reaction to the Mass in a French-speaking country. Interestingly, the contribution closes with the wish 'that Mr Ballabene will have this work engraved so that all the amateurs can render him the justice he deserves in every respect'.[4]

Further early proof of the work's reception is the harsh opinion uttered by a Spanish former Jesuit, the mathematician-musicologist Antonio Eximeno (1729–1808), who had settled in Italy after the expulsion of the Society of Jesus from Spain. In conducting a polemical debate regarding Martini's counterpoint theory in general, Eximeno seized the occasion of his 1774 *Descrizione* to launch a brusque attack against the clergyman.[5] In a 120-page pamphlet dedicated to Martini's newly published

---

2 'Una Mefsa a 24 Cori . . . parendomi impofsibile che quel uomo pofsa saper formare un Contrapunto di tal razza'; letter by Pietro Morandi to Martini, dated 18 December 1774 (I-Bc, Carteggio martiniano, I.014.081). Morandi writes from Pergola (near Urbino), where he is *maestro di cappella* and cathedral organist. It is the same region, in the upper Papal States, where Ballabene had served as *maestro* during the 1750s in several short-term employments and where he obviously was still remembered, though apparently not as a brilliant contrapuntist.

3 Letter by Domenico Morichi (Fabriano) to Martini, dated 29 April 1774 (I-Bc, Carteggio martiniano, I.002.002). In Morichi's case, too, the astonishment seems to be connected not only with the Herculean task itself but equally with the author's reputation (Ballabene in earlier years had been *maestro di cappella* at Apiro, near Fabriano).

4 'Que M. Ballabene faffe graver cet ouvrage, afin que tous les amateurs puiffent lui rendre la justice qu'il mérite à tous égards'; Anonymous ('M***'), 'Messe à 48 voix', p. 202. For the most significant passages of the article, see Document 5. As *L'esprit des journaux* was published in Liège, it is likely that one of Ballabene's former students at the Collegio Liegese (see Chapter 6, n. 13) may have arranged for the release of the tribute, possibly even on the initiative of the master himself: after all, the reference to fair recognition reads almost like an echo of Ballabene's customary complaints on the matter.

5 Unlike Ballabene's Mass, Eximeno's programmatic essay *Dell'origine e delle regole della musica colla storia del suo progresso, decadenza, e rinnovazione* (Roma: M. Barbiellini, 1774) had not at all aroused Martini's approval, who in turn had responded with his own, no less programmatic, counterpoint treatise.

Saggio fondamentale (1775), Eximeno criticises, inter alia, the fact that in dense and wordy contrapuntal textures the meaning of the sung text inevitably ends up sounding like nonsense. He cites Ballabene's Mass as a particularly bad example, calling it a creation of 'useless effort', but his brief and shallow mention of the work makes it clear that he had not seen the score.[6]

How reliable are such objections? A common feature of Ballabene's contemporary critics is indeed that most of them knew the work exclusively from hearsay, and it seems that the sheer spectre of the contrapuntal Moloch only assumed such threatening and disconcerting proportions in their imaginations. It is obvious that Eximeno's relatively clumsy criticism of Ballabene's work was directed primarily at Martini: it is a case of the sack being beaten in order to hurt the donkey. In view of Eximeno's lack of knowledge of the work itself, however, the blanket rejection of the Mass seems also to stand for the angry expression of important currents in Italian music theory whereby manifestations of traditional counterpoint were considered symbols of a hopelessly backward world view, regardless of all technical challenges they also captured.

Martini's willingness to support Ballabene's work inevitably made him a target for representatives of modern tendencies. As an exponent of the leading generation of music theorists of the time, Eximeno aligned himself with a whole host of younger colleagues, among them allies such as Vincenzo Manfredini (1737–1799) and Saverio Mattei (1742–1795). On the other hand, Martini was a lifelong advocate of church music ideals (he hailed Pisari as the 'Palestrina of the eighteenth century'), yet he was fully aware of changing times. In his own work and thought this awareness meant that he was always trying to perform a balancing act between tradition and modernity, an attempt that, notwithstanding its profound theoretical grounding, was doomed to failure.[7] As will be seen, Ballabene's historical position can be evaluated in similar terms.

Ballabene and his Mass are briefly mentioned in another work of music theory published during his lifetime, the *Elementi teorico-pratici di musica* (1791) by composer and violinist Francesco Galeazzi (1758–1819) from Turin. Galeazzi had heard of the work, but clearly was another who had not seen the score, otherwise his short description would hardly have remained limited to 'a Mass for 48 parts divided into 12 choruses, each of which proceeds autonomously without the help of the others'. In his case, however,

---

6 See Document 6. Even though Eximeno's position proves not quite sustainable, Baini in 1808 actually takes the trouble to refute his arguments (Baini, 'Mottetto', pp. 16–18).

7 For an overview of this conflictual topic, especially among Italian theorists, see Garda et al., *La musica*, pp. 9–41.

there is no more specific value judgement beyond the more general remark of being 'a grand and marvellous work' and that 'in this manner lies the highest accomplishment of human genius which has been seen up to the present day'.[8]

As far as Charles Burney (1726–1814) is concerned, there is strong reason to believe that the Englishman never heard about Ballabene and his Mass, despite his correspondence with Martini during the 1770s.[9] In Burney's printed works there is no mention whatsoever of the composer or his work.[10]

On the other hand, another prominent figure in European music life, Georg Joseph Vogler (1749–1814) from Mannheim, knew about the Mass as early as 1780, leading him to exclaim: 'If we only had in Germany [a] few works like . . . the 16-part *Dixit Dominus* by *Pittoni* . . . the 12-choir and 48-part Mass by *Ballabene*, and the like'.[11] In 1773, the decisive year with regard to Ballabene's cause, Vogler had visited Bologna intending to study with Martini. It is quite probable that he saw with his own eyes the works he praised later in his *Betrachtungen* (1780) as brilliant examples of Italian vocal composition (including Pitoni's previously mentioned *Dixit* but also the *Miserere* settings by Gregorio Allegri and Tommaso Baj, Masses by Giacomo Antonio Perti and Martini and others). In his discourse, however, in a somewhat cursory yet also targeted presentation, Ballabene's Mass and the other prominent works are invoked as weighty examples of the superiority of the Italians over the Germans in vocal composition. For obvious reasons, Ballabene's work itself gets no further comment.[12]

8 'Una Messa a 48 voci in 12 Cori distribuite, ognun de' quali da Se si regge senza bisogno degli altri; opera insigne e maravigliosa . . . in questo genere è il maggior sforzo dell'ingegno umano fin' ora veduto'; Galeazzi, *Elementi*, vol. II, p. 276. For the quotation in its context see Document 9.

9 For Burney's letters to Martini see I-Bc, Carteggio martiniano I.001.026–30, L.117.034. For his further exchange with Italian musicians in England during the 1770s, see Ribeiro, *The Letters*, pp. 116f, 228ff, 255f. Once again, Martini's silence on this particular matter is striking.

10 Even in the preface to his 1785 *Account of the Musical Performances in Westminster-Abbey . . . In Commemoration of Handel*, in which Burney registered the largest music performances, in terms of numbers, that had taken place during the course of the previous few centuries, the rehearsal of the works by Pisari and Ballabene is not mentioned, even though Burney was aware that, 'At many other *gran funzioni* and feſtivals in Rome, Venice, and other parts of Italy, a congreſs of *two or three hundred muſicians* is not, perhaps, very uncommon'; Burney, *An account*, p. X.

11 'Hätten wir doch nur [ein] paar Arbeiten in Teutſchland aufzuweiſen, wie . . . das 16ſtimmige *Dixit Dominus* von *Pittoni* . . . die 12chörige und 48ſtimmige Meß von *Ballabene*, u.d.m.'; Vogler, *Betrachtungen*, p. 269.

12 'Denn aus den vorigen Citationen läſt [sic] es sich ſehr deutlich einſehen, um wie viel beſſer man in Wälſchland die Singkompoſition findet' (ibid., p. 270). As has been seen, Ballabene's need at times to resort to the oddest melodic and rhythmic writing in order

In contrast to Vogler's exalted assessment, other contemporary witnesses included the person behind the work in their testimonies. One of these was Johann Friedrich Reichardt (1752–1814), renowned German composer and music critic, who must have met Ballabene personally during his second Italian journey in 1790. Greatly impressed by simply encountering a composition 'for 48, that is to say: *Forty-eight* genuinely elaborated vocal parts *alla Capella*', he ordered a copy of his own to be sent to Berlin. It may have been Ballabene himself – whom Reichardt describes as a 'very elderly church composer' – who told him that the Mass had once been performed 'with extraordinary applause' and (in the words of a clearly embittered man) that in the race for the *maestro di cappella* position at St Peter's years ago, in his stead and notwithstanding his aspirations, a modern opera composer had been chosen, somebody 'who in his lifetime had not written anything *alla Capella*'.[13]

In 1812, lexicographer Ernst Ludwig Gerber (1746–1819) propagates Reichardt's narrative and retells his tale, sharing his amazement about the composition and his disappointment about Ballabene's unhappy fate. Moreover, in Gerber's version, Ballabene becomes even more of a projection screen for a glorifying transfiguration: his lack of success as an artist is romantically traced back to outstanding modesty, as Gerber describes 'his silent grandeur, his self-sufficiency, unconcerned as to whether the world knew about him, and when tribute, the well-deserved admiration, would be paid'.[14] These impressions could not have been based on any personal experience; as we have seen, Ballabene's letters reveal quite a different picture of his character.

Vogler's and Reichardt's testimonies suggest that Ballabene's Mass was received differently in Germany from the way it was received in Italy, now focusing less on theoretical aspects and more on comparison with the works

---

to compose in forty-eight parts could not really recommend his work as an appropriate example of 'how much better vocal composition can be found in Italy'. It is evident that the matchless Mass here served as part of an ideological battle rather than as an individual exemplary work with outstanding qualities throughout. At the same time, it was an item that Vogler's readers would probably never get the chance to know.

13 Reichardt, '1. Fortsetzung', p. 65. For the various quotations in their context see Document 10.
14 'Diese ſtille Gröſze, dies ſich ſelbſt Genugſeyn, unbekümmert, ob es auch die Welt weiſz, und wann ſie die verdiente Bewunderung zollen wird'; Gerber, *Neues historisch-biographisches Lexikon*, vol. I, col. 244. For the quotation in its context see Document 11. Very similar in its approach (and clearly based on Gerber) is the portrait sketched by Utto Kornmüller in 1870; see Kornmüller, *Lexikon*, p. 42.

of past and present German composers. Unlike its treatment in the Catholic
centres of the peninsula, in Germany it also encountered a largely different aesthetic and socio-cultural environment. As outlined at the beginning
of this study, in German music historicism, especially in regions marked
by Protestantism, Palestrina's model in general and polychoral works of
Roman origin, particularly those by Benevoli, were honoured as inspira-
tional sources for the creation of a new sacred concert repertoire; these
developments spanned generations until well into the 1860s. On the other
hand, the early Catholic Palestrina revival associated with names like Cas-
par Ett (1788–1847), Franz Sales Kandler (1792–1831) and Carl Proske
(1794–1861) made comparably little reference to polychorality.[15]

With the growth of musicology as an academic discipline, however, polychoral counterpoint as a historical phenomenon also became a subject of
scientific interest. In this context, Ballabene and his work were received
with much less enthusiasm. Austrian music historian Raphael Georg Kiesewetter (1834), for instance, who was the principal contact of Fortunato
Santini (1777–1861) for the exchange of sheet music with Vienna, reviewed
the Mass with a wrinkle of his nose:

> The 48-part Mass by *Ballabene* was proposed to the editor several years
> ago to be copied for his collection; he put it back, unutilised, because
> throughout he could not detect any thought in it, apart from the petty-
> minded ambition to evade fifths and octaves; obviously it cannot be
> said that there is any effect. Music has lost nothing from the fact that
> this kind of country storm has gone out of fashion.[16]

By that time, Santini in Rome was well known throughout Europe as a
music collector and also as the owner of a copy of the Mass. In fact, Santini played a key role in Ballabene's posthumous fame. In an 1842 letter he
shares his thoughts on the work, suggesting (in a statement not dissimilar to
Kiesewetter's) that 'one should not expect from it a great effect, in any performance whatsoever', clearly speculating on the basis of the score alone,

---

15 For a detailed account of the history of the movement see Garratt, *Palestrina*, pp. 133–213.
16 'Die 48stimmige Messe von *Ballabene* ist dem Herausgeber vor mehren [sic] Jahren zum
    Kopiren für seine Sammlung angeboten worden; er stellte sie unbenutzt zurück, weil er
    darin durchaus keinen Gedanken ausfindig machen konnte, wenn es nicht das kleinliche
    Streben wäre, Quinten und Oktave zu meiden; von Effekt kann da, wie natürlich, keine
    Rede sein. – Die Musik hat daran, dass diese Art Landsturm aus der Mode gekommen,
    allerdings nichts verloren'; Kandler – Kiesewetter, *Ueber das Leben*, p. 129.

if not also on oral tradition.[17] August Wilhelm Ambros (who was Kiesewetter's nephew) in his *Geschichte der Musik* (1878) utters discreetly that the Mass 'was performed at Rome in 1774 [sic] with dubious success'; it seems that he knew the composition and its history only superficially, referring to the existence of the manuscript 'in Santini's collection'.[18] Music bibliographer Robert Eitner, in 1900, gives sober notice of the twelve-choir *Kyrie* and *Gloria* and mentions Heiberger's *Lettera* but not the rehearsal.[19] Eventually, in his 1910 study on Santini's music collection, Joseph Killing sweepingly denounces Ballabene's polychoral writing: 'In musical terms, these works are entirely grounded in the outgoing eighteenth century and cannot claim any significance'. And regarding the twelve-choir Mass he specifies: 'Most of all Santini's patience is to be admired, as he copied the work in a huge format – the score is 59 cm wide and 81 cm high'.[20] Musicologist Karl Gustav Fellerer's lapidary comment (1929) is in line with this general consensus when he states: 'Despite all craftsmanship, this Mass gives the impression of a spirited experiment rather than an effective work of art'.[21]

Twentieth-century music dictionaries and handbooks basically perpetuate the mainly disapproving message of these later opinions whereby Ballabene's Mass is considered (to put it bluntly) the bizarre product of a musical eccentric that deserves no deeper involvement. Consequently, there has been no close study dedicated to the work until now.

---

17 'Non [è] da ripromettersene un grande effetto nella qualunque sia esecuzione'; letter to François-Joseph Fétis, dated 17 February 1842. For the quotation in its context see Document 13.

18 'Der letzte, späte Nachzügler dieser ganzen Richtung [i. e. polychorischer Componisten], der Römer Gregorio Ballabene, gehört erst der zweiten Hälfte des 18. Säculums an – [er componierte] ein 16stimmiges Dixit, eine Messe zu zwölf Chören mit 48 Stimmen – letztere wurde 1774 in Rom mit zweifelhaftem Erfolg aufgeführt (diese Arbeiten kamen später in Santini's Sammlung)'; Ambros, *Geschichte*, vol. IV (1878), p. 117f; 3rd edn (1909), vol. IV, p. 153.

19 Eitner, *Biographisch-bibliogaphisches Quellen-Lexikon*, vol. V (1901), p. 84; on Ballabene see also ibid., vol. I (1900), p. 316, and vol. X (1904), p. 373.

20 'Musikalisch stehen diese Werke ganz auf dem Boden des ausgehenden 18. Jahrhunderts und können keinerlei Wert beanspruchen'; 'Zu bewundern ist hier am meisten die Geduld Santinis, der in einem Riesenformat – die Partitur ist 59 cm breit und 81 cm hoch – das Werk abschrieb'; Killing, *Kirchenmusikalische Schätze*, p. 167. This judgement must be one of the reasons why Killing did not place any of Ballabene's works among his series of editions of 'Sacred Music Treasures from the Library of the Abbate Fortunato Santini', which make up the majority of his study.

1 'Trotz aller Kunstfertigkeit macht diese Messe mehr den Eindruck eines geistvollen Experiments als eines wirksamen Kunstwerks'; Fellerer, *Der Palestrinastil*, p. 212.

Considered within the larger context of music history, the forty-eight-part Mass has attracted interest primarily as an oddity, an object of curiosity – apart from its unfortunate role among Ballabene's Italian contemporaries as a virtual projection screen for disparaging its author and the spirit of the age he seemed to represent. From the beginning, its significance lay mainly in the theoretical realm, as a means to expound the idea that twelve-choir composition in real parts fully compliant with classical counterpoint rules was within practical human powers. It also became a special kind of souvenir of Rome for fervent music lovers.

Among the performers, researchers, composers, collectors and music enthusiasts who have discovered the Mass, none appears to have considered it a subject of profound analysis or historical study. Composers such as Reichardt, Baini, Nicolai, Tommaso Giordani (1730/33–1806), Johann Simon Mayr (1763–1845) and Bernhard Klein (1793–1832) possessed their own copies of the score. And so did music collectors such as Santini, Georg Poelchau (1773–1836) and Siegfried Wilhelm Dehn (1799–1858), the Irish priest Richard Kenrick (1781–1827), the Russian diplomat Aleksandr Jakovlevič Skarjatin (1815–1884) and the German anatomist Guido Richard Wagener (1822–1896). Most of the eight extant copies of Ballabene's Mass, manuscripts datable largely between 1772 and 1858, are connected with these names.[22]

---

22 Copies in B-Bc, D-B, I-Bc (two copies), I-BGc, I-Rama, I-Rc and RUS-Mk; see Appendix II. The whereabouts of the copy once owned by Giordani and later by Kenrick is presently unknown (in the 1827 auction of Kenrick's collection the volume was sold to an unidentified buyer). For the background to the case see Sharpe, 'Tommaso Giordani', p. 32. Also Reichardt's copy from the early 1790s (see Document 10) has not yet been identified. The score in D-B, dated 'ROMA MDCCCXXV', a somewhat inaccurate copy in Santini's hand, comes from the collection of Georg Poelchau, whose bookplate and inscription it bears (a score of Ballabene's Mass is first recorded in Poelchau's handwritten catalogue, vol. IV, dated 8 May 1832; see D-B, Mus. MS theor. Kat. 41, f. 31v). Eitner in 1900, however, locates two copies in Berlin: one at the Königliche Bibliothek ('B.B., MS 1070', most probably the copy today in D-B, Mus.MS 1070) and another one in the collections of the Sing-Akademie; see Eitner, *Biographisch-bibliographisches Quellen-Lexikon*, vol. I (1900), p. 316. The latter of the two is missing. Bernhard Klein's copy of the work (almost certainly obtained from Santini in Rome) is mentioned in the register of the manuscripts he acquired during his Italian honeymoon in 1824/1825 (Scheideler, *Komponieren*, p. 562); the whereabouts of the score is uncertain, yet the document may be linked with the score later owned by Wagener (clearly marked as part of his library) and kept today in B-Bc (see Appendix II, no. 7.1). Otto Nicolai explicitly affirms having ordered his copy of the *Kyrie* and *Gloria* by 'Giorgio Ballabene' from Santini in Rome (Nicolai, 'Italienische Studien', p. 52). The copy now in I-Rama carries a corresponding entry in Nicolai's handwriting dated 20 September 1835 and signed 'O. N.' (Figure 12.2). The partial copy in I-BGc is referred to as part of Mayr's estate; the one in I-Rc comes from Baini's. Several copies bear a reference to the collection of Santini, who produced a number of duplicates (besides the one in I-Rama, also those in D-B and RUS-Mk). At his death, Dehn is said to have left

None of these figures linked to copies seems to have attempted to arrange a performance of the work.[23]

After Ballabene's death, his Mass was met with increasing amazement, with little consideration of its technical and artistic merits. As a composition without a documented performance history, it was generally treated like a singular musical monument of a distant past and – not only in view of its physical dimensions – with the monolithic aura of an enigmatic museum object. The question of whether or not the work was a creation of 'useless effort' (Eximeno, 1775) was no longer asked.

As far as nineteenth-century press reviews are concerned, the most note-worthy mention of the Mass occurs in relation to the 1892 Internationale Ausstellung für Musik- und Theaterwesen in Vienna, where the score was exhibited by the Italian national section as a 'treasure' and curious item of Roman music history, an outstanding element of marvel and fascination.[24]

---

a (today unidentified) score of the Mass, explicitly referred to as copied by Dehn himself (Scholz, 'Siegfried Wilhelm Dehn. Nekrolog', p. 163). The copy in RUS-Mk belonged to the estate of Skarjatin (who had acquired it from Santini in Rome). According to the library catalogue in I-Bc, the second copy there (dated 1811) originates from a nineteenth-century private collection from the Bologna area ('copia posseduta una volta dal Marchese Barto-lomeo can[oni]co Rusconi di Cento'). The first Bolognese copy appears to be Ballabene's officially submitted autograph score. Another partial copy mentioned in the catalogue of I-Fc (*Christe eleison* only) is missing.

According to Fétis, the score of Ballabene's Mass was capitalised on by Santini, who sold his duplicates 'at a price of ten Roman scudi' ('On peut obtenir du même amateur [Santini] des copies de la grande messe à quarante-huit voix, moyennant le prix de dix écus romains'; Fétis, *Biographie universelle*, vol. II, p. 50 [2nd rev. edn, vol. I., p. 231]). Even Fétis himself ordered a copy from Santini, who in 1842 confided to him his opinion regard-ing the work; see Fétis, *Correspondance*, pp. 172–173; furthermore Document 13. Neither Fétis's correspondence nor his writings reveal whether the manuscript was ever delivered.

23 During the nineteenth century, Pisari's *Dixit Dominus* was also in circulation in private collections – as a sought-after *Kunstkammer* object. Not only did Poelchau in Berlin pos-sess a copy of the score, as testified by his catalogue dated 1832 (D-B, Mus. MS theor. Kat. 41, f. 114v), but also other collectors, like Anton Friedrich Justus Thibaut (d. 1840), law professor at Heidelberg and founder of the local Singverein (see *Verzeichniss*, p. 27, n. 432; copy today in D-Mbs, Mus.MS 999) and Franconian baron Franz Wilhelm von Ditfurth (1801–1880; copy dated 1834, today in D-Mbs, Mus.MS 2959). Kiesewetter's copy, realised by Santini in 1833, is in A-Wn (SA.67.G.16 MUS MAG). A '118-page clean score' of the work ('Saubere Partitur. 118 Seiten.') furthermore appears in the 1857 auction catalogue of the Berlin musicologist Carl von Winterfeld's (1784–1852) music collection (Friedländer, *Carl von Winterfeld's*, p. 17, n. 645). And, of course, Santini also owned a copy (today in D-MÜs, SANT Hs 3210).

24 Wartenegg, 'Die Wiener internationale Ausstellung', p. 227; Heuberger, 'Internation-ale Ausstellung', p. 2. Heuberger refers to the Italian exhibits as 'truly tremendous treasures . . . which would certainly have increased considerably if ecclesiastical Rome had not ostentatiously declined any participation' ('geradezu ungeheuere Schätze . . . die

Another important press record concerns a partial performance of the work, the only known reference to which is by Grell, who reported in 1886 that he 'once heard the Kyrie in Milan'; unfortunately, he gives no further details.[25] Nothing more explicit about this event has come to light.[26]

gewiß noch bedeutend zugenommen hätten, wenn fich das kirchliche Rom nicht oftentativ ferngehalten hätte'). Again, in both press reports the mention of the Mass avoids any comment or qualifying adjective. According to the exhibition catalogue, the manuscript copy 'in Fol[io] max[imo]' solemnly presented to the international audience was a loan by the 'R. Bibl. S. Cecilia' (Berwin and Hirschfeld, *Internationale Ausstellung*, p. 133). It is most likely that this was the same source as the one now housed in I-Rama, which is bound (presumably for the purposes of the exhibition) in a taupe-coloured full cloth hard cover bearing the royal coat of arms in gold together with the inscription 'R[EGIA] ACCADEMIA DI S. CECILIA | IN ROMA | BIBLIOTECA', the name of the composer and the title of the work (see Appendix II, no. 11).

25 'Aus Ballabene's sogar achtundvierzigstimmiger Messe habe ich das Kyrie einst in Mailand gehört'; Wichmann, 'Das größte Musik-Kunststück', p. 1131. In the archival materials in I-Mfd regarding the appointment procedure of the new *maestro di cappella* at Milan Cathedral in 1779, no works by Ballabene related to his candidacy are extant. There are furthermore no indications at all that Ballabene might have sent the Mass to Milan in the course of the selection process (as it would appear, his candidacy was limited to a letter of recommendation and a certified list of his merits; see Document 7a–b). The papers submitted by his competitor Jannacconi, on the other hand, also contained in the I-Mfd file, include several autograph compositions by Jannacconi.

26 Another equally questionable reference to a performance of Ballabene's work is attributed to Siegfried Wilhelm Dehn (who had visited Italy in 1844) and quoted in his American obituary (1858): 'Dehn sometimes described to us the performance of that Mass as he once heard it in Italy'; A. W. T., 'Sketch of Prof. Dehn', p. 261).

12   The history of the score

In the absence of any actual performance history of Ballabene's Mass, a complementary reception history of the score can be briefly explored. In respect to its dissemination, two points of focus are necessary.

First, there is the composer himself, living in Rome until at least 1797.[1] There is no doubt that after 1776 Ballabene would have continued to preserve and spread the memory of his *chef-d'oeuvre*, especially among younger musicians who came to Rome as visitors or for study purposes. Therefore, it is very likely that Reichardt (as his brief report on Ballabene seems to reveal) obtained his copy thanks to a face-to-face encounter he had with the composer, who provided a first-hand (though probably not totally objective) testimony regarding the 'premiere' of his Mass (see Document 10). The partial score left by Mayr, copied by an unidentified writer, may have a similar history.[2] The full autograph Ballabene must have kept for his own library is missing, and there is no indication as to the whereabouts of his estate.

All further extant scores share a second line of descent. As has already been outlined, as early as 1774 Padre Martini, as guardian of the score that Ballabene had presented to the Accademia Filarmonica, was contacted by interested *maestri di cappella* eager to obtain a copy of the work and to gain an idea of its uniqueness. It is fair to assume that Martini (and in later years his successor) entrusted professional copyists of his scriptorium with

---

1 His name appears in the archives of the Congregazione di Santa Cecilia until summer 1797; see I-Raanc, 'Verbale della congregazione segreta'. After that date there is no information relating to his whereabouts.

2 Mayr visited Rome several times, but all after Ballabene's death (1808, 1814, 1818). The Bergamo copy therefore must have come into his possession through one or more intermediaries. Considering the fact that Baini's partial copy is substantially congruent with the one owned by Mayr, a common provenance for both may be assumed (Appendix II, nos. 13 and 14).

DOI: 10.4324/9781003226710-13

the reproduction of the score (or parts of it) or allowed interested persons to copy from it. One of the two manuscripts in I-Bc, in fact, appears to be of such origin (see Chapter 11, n. 22), whereas the other one is most probably Ballabene's official specimen.

The three copies in I-Rama, B-Bc and D-B are all clearly signed as 'descendants' of the score that Santini had received from Bologna. The score in I-Rama (which Santini sold to Nicolai in 1835) bears an inscription in German that recapitulates this provenance ('From the collection of the renowned Abbate Fortunato Santini at Rome who had obtained it from Bologna, where the composer . . . had sent a copy of this great work'),[3] thus seeming to suggest that it might be the master copy; however, the scores in B-Bc and D-B (those from Wagener's and Poelchau's collections), both dated 1825, are also explicitly marked as being 'From the Music Collection

---

3 'Aus der Sammlung des bekannten *Abbate Fortunato Santini* zu *Rom*, welcher es aus *Bologna* erhalten hatte, wohin der Componiſt . . . eine Kopie dieſer großen Arbeit geſandt hatte'; I-Rama, A. MS 316, title page. The author of this note, signed 'O. N.', is 25-year-old Otto Nicolai (see Chapter 11, n. 22), who furthermore admits, 'I acquired it from Santini on 20 September 1835 in Rome' ('Ich erſtand es von *Santini* am 20ᵗ *Septᵇʳ* 1835 in *Rom*'; see Figure 12.2). It is likely that many of the scores Nicolai purchased in Italy were sent to Germany via the Prussian embassy, where he was employed as an organist (February 1834 to March 1836), or through others of his German contacts in Rome (Scheideler, *Komponieren*, p. 247). In the case of the Ballabene Mass, the format may have turned out to be a problem, which is why Nicolai supposedly left the bulky object in Rome when departing for Macerata – Bologna – Milan – Vienna in July 1836. According to his diary, at his return to Rome in November 1838 he was so short of money that he had to sell all his items of value to make ends meet (Altmann, *Otto Nicolais Tagebücher*, p. 193ff). These circumstances might explain why the score (an unfolded 21-page volume in a format of 78 × 54 cm) remained in Rome at his second departure in September 1839.

At his very first arrival at Rome in February 1834, Nicolai had carried with him a wish list made by Berlin collector Poelchau ('das mir mitgegebene Pro Memoria-Zettelchen'; letter to Poelchau, dated 10 March 1834, see Vierneisel, 'Otto Nicolai', pp. 229–230). When reporting back to him in September 1835, Nicolai mentions that Ballabene's Mass and a sixteen-part *Dixit Dominus* by Pitoni are among the newly purchased works (for the letter, dated sectionwise 14, 18, 20, 21, 22 September 1835, see Vierneisel, 'Otto Nicolai', p. 230ff). Later, in February 1837, Nicolai confirms that he has obtained these two works from Santini (Nicolai, 'Italienische Studien', p. 52). The extant score of Ballabene's Mass that originates from Poelchau's collection (D-B, Mus.MS 1070) is dated 1825, meaning that this copy is probably not one of the manuscripts that Nicolai collected in Rome (the Berlin score, however, was copied by Santini, apparently from the manuscript that today is in I-Rama, A. MS 316. It must have joined Poelchau's library through other intermediaries, as Nicolai's did not arrive; see Appendix II, no. 8). As indicated earlier, the Nicolai copy of the Mass can be identified as the one today in I-Rama, A. MS 316; the whereabouts of the corresponding *Dixit Dominus* by Pitoni, however, is unknown (Scheideler, *Komponieren*, p. 555). Supposedly, this score never arrived in Berlin either (there is no trace of it, neither in Poelchau's catalogue nor in the library holdings of D-B and D-Bsa).

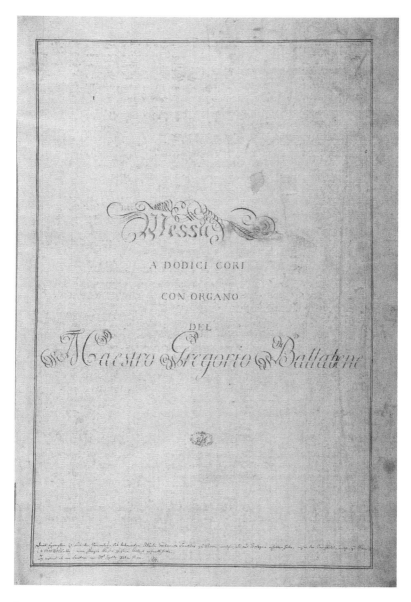

Figure 12.1 Gregorio Ballabene, *Messa a dodici cori* (I-Rama, A. MS. 316), title page.

Detail: Handwritten note by Otto Nicolai: 'Dies Exemplar ift aus der Sammlung des bekannten *Abbate Fortunato Santini* zu *Rom*, welcher es aus *Bologna* erhalten hatte, wohin der Componift, welcher zu Rom | († *circa* 1800) lebte, eine Kopie diefer großen Arbeit gefandt hatte. | Ich erftand es von *Santini* am 20ᵗ *Septᵇʳ* 1835 in *Rom*. | O. N.'

of Mr Abbate Fortunato Santini'.[4] Furthermore, a copy of the Mass is still documented as being part of Santini's collection more than a century later, in 1929.[5]

In 1835, Nicolai informed Poelchau that Santini had entrusted his own copy to him, while keeping the score he had produced on Nicolai's behalf (which, as far as Nicolai was concerned, might have contained errors). This particular favour seems to have cost the young German an extra fee.[6] It would be very surprising indeed if Santini, as a collector, had sold this particular manuscript that was in such high demand by other music enthusiasts. An item of such rarity and eccentricity (not only in terms of content but also in terms of its enormous format) would require particular materials and a special effort to realise – it would also allow him to ask a significant price.

---

4 'Dalla Collezione musicale del Signor Abbate Fortunato Santini' (B-Bc, FOLIO-17250; D-B, Mus. MS 1070, title page). The contacts between the Berlin Sing-Akademie and Santini in Rome had been established years before Nicolai's visit. In 1837 Santini was even appointed honorary member of the Sing-Akademie, a sign of approval and gratitude (Rostirolla, 'Musica antica', p. 8).

5 Fellerer, *Die musikalischen Schätze*, p. 16. The 1929 exhibition catalogue is the last proof of the existence of the score as part of the collection. A year earlier, in 1928, the score had been mentioned by Hüntemann (Hüntemann, *Die Messen*, pp. 6, 52). The work is also listed in Killing's 1910 study (Killing, *Kirchenmusikalische Schätze*, p. 475). In Fellerer's 1931 catalogue the work is no longer registered (Fellerer, 'Verzeichnis'), and neither does it appear in the typewritten catalogue by Wörmann, compiled in the 1950s (Wörmann, [Catalogue]).

6 'Ich habe Santini sein Exemplar abgekauft u. ihm die neue Abschrift, in die sich vielleicht Fehler geschlichen, gelassen. Aber theuer!'; Nicolai in his letter to Poelchau dated 20 September 1835 (reproduced in Vierneisel, 'Otto Nicolai', p. 234). Already a few days earlier, on 18 September, Nicolai had confessed, regarding Santini: 'By the way, he is a bit avaricious and vain also' ('Uebrigens ist er auch ein wenig geldgierig und auch eitel', ibid., p. 232).

This price, as Fétis reveals, amounted to the impressive sum of ten Roman scudi – for eleven sheets (twenty-one pages) of music.[7]

The Mass seems to have been one of Santini's bestselling collectables, considering the fact that Fétis, Klein and Skarjatin also obtained (or at least ordered) their copies from him.[8] It is obvious that Santini and his duplicates play a key role in the distribution history of the score, and we should not be surprised if further nineteenth-century copies of Ballabene's Mass originating from his workshop eventually come to light.

---

7 For Fétis, see Chapter 11, n. 22. Santini's business sense is furthermore thematised by Nicolai, who on 10 July 1835 noted in his diary: 'In the afternoon I was at the home of Santini, who makes a friendly face when you give him an order to copy music', and the day after he adds: 'An afternoon visit to Santini's house, to diligently look through music to let him copy now, in order to bring back something good with me' ('Nachmittag war ich bei Santini, der ein freundliches Gesicht macht, wenn man von ihm Musik kopieren läßt'; 'Nachmittags Besuch bei Santini, von dem ich jetzt fleißig Musik durchsehen und abschreiben lassen will, um etwas Gutes mitzubringen'; Altmann, *Otto Nicolais Tagebücher*, p. 127). The Ballabene Mass is not mentioned in Nicolai's diary, not even around 20 September 1835, the day of purchase.

To contextualise the value of ten Roman scudi, it is worth noting that in November 1835 Nicolai paid a monthly rent of eight scudi for an apartment that he proudly describes as consisting of 'a pretty bedroom on the sunny side and a large living room towards the front on the north side; I pay eight scudi a month. So I have moved up!' In 1839, Nicolai charged one scudo for a music lesson ('ein hübsches Schlafzimmer auf der Sonnenseite und ein großes Zimmer nach vorn heraus auf der Nordseite; ich zahle acht scudi monatlich. Also habe ich mich zugelegt!'; 'Ich gebe ungefähr täglich 3 Stunden zu 1 Scudo'; Altmann, *Otto Nicolais Tagebücher*, pp. 146, 196). In a letter to his father dated 3 and 28 October 1835, however, Nicolai describes his new apartment quite differently ('Heute habe ich ein neues kleines Quartier (1 Stube und 1 Kammer, beide klein, aber auf der Sonnenseite, was bei Römischen Stuben ohne Ofen für den Winter viel Wert ist) bezogen, um 1 Scudo monatlich an der Miete zu sparen. Hier zahle ich 5 Scudi (7½ Taler); früher 6'; Altmann, *Otto Nicolai. Briefe*, p. 153).

8 It was noted earlier that Klein's score was copied by 1824/1825 at the latest, whereas in February 1842 Fétis still had not received the one he had ordered (Document 13). Skarjatin arrived in Rome only in 1843, where he worked at the Russian embassy as first political secretary until 1858. From about 1847 onwards, he paid Santini a monthly salary of five scudi for copying music for his own collection, whereas the earliest extant copies carry the date 1844 (Janitzek, 'Santini', pp. 224–225; Féderov, 'V. V. Stasov', p. 60). The 'Santini-Skarjatin-Collection' in RUS-Mk is basically the result of this cooperation, its surviving legacy amounting to ninety volumes of about 400 pages each (medium format: 28 × 22 cm). The collection, however, also contains many works with a provenance other than Santini's studio (Malinina, 'Santini's Collection', p. 146). The library catalogue gives no more specific information regarding the Ballabene manuscript and its content (Medvedeva and Sigida, 'Аннотированный указатель' [Annotated index], pp. 13, 28). The score is part of the last volume of the collection – vol. 90 – and has been folded three times from a page format of 72 × 61 cm to 21.5 × 31 cm (I am indebted to Mrs Irina Brezhneva, director of the manuscript department of the Moscow Conservatoire Library, for this information).

The provenance of the Giordani-Kenrick copy is as yet largely unknown, and so is its current location.[9] By contrast, it is reasonable to suggest that the score of Ballabene's Mass, which Dehn (in Berlin) copied for himself, was based either on the score his teacher Klein had brought from Rome in 1824/1825 or on the one Poelchau had obtained in the mid-1830s.[10]

Even now it remains unclear when exactly Santini came into possession of his own 'master copy'. The catalogue of his collection, printed in 1820,[11] in which 'La gran Messa a 48' is registered under Ballabene's name, may signal the *terminus ante quem* from having received it. It has already been mentioned that according to 'O. N.' this manuscript came from Bologna (see n. 3). Unfortunately, Santini's correspondence with Bologna from these years has not yet come to light.[12] In any case, the date 'MDCCCXXV' inscribed in the manuscript from Wagener's collection (the score in B-Bc) most likely refers to the year when Santini copied that score, not when the Mass first entered his collection.

What is certain is that Santini knew Ballabene personally, even during his childhood, as Ballabene taught counterpoint at the orphanage where Santini

9 Given that Giordani (1730/1733–1806) spent his life (from the 1750s onwards) in London and Dublin, the score will have come to him through an intermediary. When in 1827 the item appears in the auction of Kenrick's estate (Kenrick being the priest who had purchased the manuscript at the sale of Giordani's library around 1801), the promotional text refers to a written note in the score ('It is the Chef d'Oeuvre of Ballabene, Maestro di Capella at Bologna, and was made by him, as an Ex-voto, or accomplishment of a vow for some certain providential deliverance, as is testified at the end'). This information could hardly be ascribable to Santini or to Ballabene himself, but at the very most to a clever agent or simply to a bad translation from the Italian. Sharpe, who was the first to draw attention to this case, suggests Dr John Troy (1739–1823) as Giordani's contact person. Troy was an Irish Dominican and future Archbishop of Dublin who lived in Rome from 1756 to 1776, where he could well have obtained a copy of the then already renowned composition (Sharpe, 'Tommaso Giordani', pp. 30–35).

10 It is known that Dehn visited Santini's collection in Rome in 1844 (Janitzek, 'Santini', p. 220). In his obituary, however, the score is registered among the works copied 'most gracefully' by himself ('von ihm selbst höchst sauber und zierlich geschriebene Copieen'; Scholz, 'Siegfried Wilhelm Dehn. Nekrolog', p. 163). Therefore, it may be doubted that Dehn would pass days if not weeks of his Roman stay copying a work that he probably had at his disposal in Berlin and that furthermore would turn out difficult to transport home safely. Dehn's clean copy of the work, 'equal to the finest specimens of printing', is also mentioned in his American obituary in *Dwight's Journal of Music* (A. W. T., 'Sketch of Prof. Dehn', p. 261). On Poelchau's copy see Appendix II, note 10.

11 *Catalogo della musica esistente presso Fortunato Santini in Roma Nel Palazzo de' Principi Odescalchi incontro la Chiesa de' SS. XII. Apostoli* (Rome: P. Salviucci, 1820).

12 Santini's 121 extant letters to the Bologna music librarian Gaetano Gaspari in I-Bc cover only the period from 1848 to 1861 (De Salvo Fattor, *Epistolario*).

grew up.[13] We do not know how the relationship between the two evolved, but it should be considered possible that Santini in later years was allowed to copy the Mass from Ballabene's own score (thus contradicting Nicolai's assertion that Santini 'had obtained it from Bologna'). No doubt future research will yield new insights about Santini's Bolognese contacts.

The whereabouts of Santini's own copy is, however, not known. Despite its appearance in the 1820 printed catalogue, the Mass is not registered in Vladimir Stasov's 1854 'Extrait du catalogue Santini';[14] it is even missing from Santini's own later manuscript catalogue (1848).[15] Ambros (1878) refers to Santini's collection – yet not very credibly – when talking about the Mass.[16] According to Killing, the score, together with several other Ballabene works, was still a documented part of the Santini collection at the Diözesanbibliothek Münster in the early twentieth century.[17] The last record dates from June 1929, when the manuscript was one of the highlights of an exhibition organised by Münster University library on occasion of the Westphalian music festival that year.[18] Today, this score is no longer extant.

---

13 'Gregorio Ballabene, che io ho conosciuto, quando io era ben piccolo nell'Orfanotrofio Romano, efsendovi Alunno, e dove il Ballabene era degnifsimo Maestro di Contrapunto' ('Gregorio Ballabene, whom I met when I was very young in the Roman Orphanage, being a pupil there, and where Ballabene was a worthy Master of Counterpoint'); Santini in a letter to Gaetano Gaspari in Bologna, dated 21 June 1852 (I-Bc, Epistolario Gaspari-Santini). Santini, born 5 January 1777, entered the orphanage at the church of Santa Maria in Aquiro in Rome on 27 June 1784 and passed to the Collegio Salviati on 11 May 1794 (Engelhardt, 'Santini in Rom', p. 12).

14 The extract of the catalogue is part of Wladimir Stassoff [sic], *L'Abbé Santini et sa collection musicale à Rome* (Florence: F. le Monnier, 1854), pp. 39–65. The prominent Russian art critic Vladimir Stasov (1824–1906) passed the years between 1851 and 1854 in Italy, mostly in Florence and Rome. During this period he employed Santini to copy an enormous number of works from his collection. The documentation collected by Rostirolla regarding Santini's relationship with the Russian intellectual contains no indication that Stasov might have acquired a copy of Ballabene's Mass. The composer's name does not appear in the index of the Stasov collection in RU-Mk (about 400 works, not only by Italian authors); Rostirolla, 'Passione', p. 436ff; see furthermore Féderov, 'V. V. Stasov', p. 61.

15 'Compendiato della musica che si trova in Roma (in partitura) presso l'abate Fortunato Santini, via dell'Anima 50, secondo piano'(I-Rama, MS 1650); transcribed in Rostirolla, 'Musica antica', pp. 27–56.

16 See Chapter 11, n. 18. Ambros (1816–1876) went to Rome in spring 1868, years after the Santini collection had been dispatched to Münster, in 1862.

17 Killing even gives the exact dimensions of the score, suggesting he had the occasion to measure it ('die Partitur ist 59 cm breit und 81 cm hoch'; Killing, *Kirchenmusikalische Schätze*, p. 167). In this respect, the score clearly differs from all the other extant copies (Appendix II, no. 6).

18 Fellerer, *Die musikalischen Schätze*, p. 16. In Fellerer's 1931 catalogue the work is not mentioned (Fellerer, 'Verzeichnis').

13 Unfortunate anachronism or accomplishment of the Roman Baroque?

As a contrapuntal vocal work for forty-eight parts in twelve choruses, Ballabene's *Kyrie* and *Gloria in excelsis* stands alone in music history. At the same time, its historical significance is not easy to determine. What at first glance may appear to be something halfway between a megalomaniac anachronism and an enlightened accomplishment of the Roman Baroque at closer inspection turns out to be neither.

Ballabene's Mass is without doubt the sophisticated fruit of a very particular mind, and there is no other musical work with which it can be properly compared. As the expression of extraordinary personal ambition and combinatorial creativity, it reveals the special talent of a composer able to conceive and pursue a project of astronomical dimensions – a capacity that must have seemed a threat to some of Ballabene's colleagues and yet that could even be perceived as a curse or obsession.[1]

The result of this project is, at any rate, outstanding. By assimilating the compositional knowledge of several preceding generations, Ballabene accomplished both an experiment and a demonstration, his foremost intention being to refute the alleged impossibility of a performable vocal texture

---

1 At this point it might be noted that Ballabene, besides his overzealous approach towards anything regarding his Mass and his tendency to complain loudly about discrimination, seems to have been a brash personality whose importunity led him to make discourteous gestures, apparently without noticing, even towards those who would actually be disposed to grant him support (see, for example, his letter to Martini, dated 26 January 1774, in I-Bc, Carteggio martiniano I.030.061; furthermore, the subtle note Sabbatini communicates to Martini on 25 June 1774, in I-Bc, Carteggio martiniano, I.016.049, or Cardinal Albani's request to Martini dated 24 July 1773, in I-Bc, Carteggio martiniano, I.015.054). Such personality traits, not uncommon in various mental disorders, may to some extent be linked to Ballabene's lack of career success. His case does indeed evoke associations with the phenomena of high giftedness and outstanding technical or scientific achievement in connection with peculiar personalities such as, for example, chess player Bobby Fischer (1943–2008) or mathematician Grigori Perelman (b. 1966).

DOI: 10.4324/9781003226710-14

in forty-eight real parts. It has to be emphasised that this demonstration-experiment was successful, at least on a theoretical level, and yet it did not result in a career breakthrough for the composer, apart from a giving him a certain notoriety and recognition.

Regarding its intellectual breeding ground, there is no factual evidence to attribute its origins to tendencies associated today with the Enlightenment (or the age of reason), during which authority and traditional beliefs in the fields of science, education, philosophy and society were questioned and were progressively replaced by rationality and personal conscientiousness. It was an age driven by people who, as Peter Gay put it, 'were men of hope because the age forced hope upon them' but also by those who 'ridiculed superstition, deplored fanaticism, extolled humanitarianism, admired science'.[2] In the case of Rome in particular, the judgement came off easily, given that the Papal States were one of the last territories in Europe successfully to oppose illuminist tendencies, adopting the zeitgeist only through violent subjugation in the course of Italian unification. It can be argued that the work by Ballabene, a man who is not known to have ever left the Papal States or to have cultivated progressive ideas in any way, is hardly the product of a mind that consciously reflects such tendencies. On the contrary, his work appears firmly to reject the reform thinking of its time rather than assimilating it in any way.

In the eighteenth century, the loss of Tridentine spirit in combination with a decay of intellectual vigour in papal Rome brought the entire state to the point of collapse – a development in which the 1773 suppression of the Jesuit order, enforced by European powers, represented only one particularly visible step on the way towards the end of the *ancien régime*. In comparison with other European capitals, eighteenth-century Rome was no longer an intellectual centre of international significance.[3] Epochal developments that had guided other states through an 'Era of Pagan Christianity' towards 'modern Paganism' (Gay) were still dimly perceptible on the Roman horizon in Ballabene's lifetime, all the more so as they were not really welcome.[4] So where, if not in papal Rome, could a church composer

2 Gay, *The Enlightenment*, pp. 24–25.
3 As Hanns Gross puts it, 'Rome struggled in vain on the intellectual and religious plane to meet the new challenges following the end of the baroque, despite bold but inadequately organized and supported efforts to confront the problems' (Gross, *Rome*, p. 285). For contextualising observations regarding the evolution of intellectual life in seventeenth- and eighteenth-century Rome and the role of Jansenism in particular, see Gross, *Rome*, pp. 247–285.
4 Gay, *The Rise*, pp. 256–321, 505. Gay's concept of the 'Era of Pagan Christianity' even focuses on centuries preceding 1700, which makes the particular backwardness of Rome (the veritable tail light of Europe) all the more apparent.

such as Ballabene – whose stylistic approach was the most conservative imaginable – be successful?

The assumption that faithfully reproducing (if not exceeding) Palestrina's model could have continued to flourish in this apparently stagnant spiritual, political and social climate can easily be refuted. Contrapuntists like Ballabene or Jannacconi did not succeed in being engaged as *maestri di cappella* at St Peter's (Jannacconi failed even twice), whereas representatives of stylistic modernity were chosen instead.[5] This circumstance should be regarded as confirmation that, even in Rome and at the most prominent Christian church, at the end of the eighteenth century there was a preference for sacred music that openly reflected progressive tendencies. A use of smaller-scaled textures (in terms of real parts), a predilection for concertato style and fewer complex contrapuntal settings are some of the manifestations of these developments. The skill and culture of contrapuntal writing, on the other hand, was increasingly limited to modern forms, which were placed alongside classical repertoire (Palestrina, Victoria, Morales etc.) and single polychoral works – rarely performed except on the most prominent feast days, 29 June (St Peter and St Paul) and 18 November (dedication of the basilica). At these events, individual musical highlights by Benevoli and Pitoni continued to be cultivated long after 1800.[6]

The modern observer of Ballabene's Mass can recognise in it (even if viewing it outside its context) more than a condensed musical intelligence and superhuman industriousness and far more than a shallow effort to provoke amazement through complexity. The work's technical and conceptual

---

5 After Antonio Boroni, who directed the Cappella Giulia from 1778 to 1792, the role was entrusted to other renowned opera composers, first to Pietro Alessandro Guglielmi, followed by Nicola Antonio Zingarelli (1804). It is significant that, only after Zingarelli's resignation in 1813, the now 73-year-old Jannacconi was appointed 'maestro supplente' (!) as a kind of bread of mercy. He exercised this role until his death in 1816, when again a prominent opera composer, Valentino Fioravanti, was appointed; he died in office in 1837.

6 Jannacconi's polychoral works, on the other hand, did not enter the canon of festive performances, whereas a sixteen-part *Dixit Dominus* by Pitoni, for instance, was performed as late as 29 June 1817 (Kantner, '*Aurea Luce*', p. 157; regarding the further development of the repertoire in the last decades of the eighteenth century, see ibid., p. 32ff). Towards the twentieth century, however, all seicento relics of the polychoral tradition seem to disappear (Rostirolla, *La Cappella Giulia*, vol. II, p. 1027ff). The last clear record of the copying of a sixteen-part *Dixit Dominus* by Pitoni dates from 31 May 1857, and this was probably for the celebrations on 29 June of that year (ibid., p. 1029). A *Dixit Dominus* by Pitoni was copied even as late as June 1906 (ibid., p. 1183); in this case, however, the number of real parts is not indicated, hence the piece cannot be fully identified. For similar nineteenth-century tendencies towards a splitting up of Renaissance and contemporary works in the repertoire of the Cappella Pontifica (where polychorality never played a significant role), see De Salvo Fattor, *La Cappella Musicale*, pp. 149–199.

qualities, outlined earlier, ultimately render these kinds of arguments untenable, especially since, as we have seen, many derogatory judgements of the past were made without knowledge of the score. And there is also another level of significance to the piece. In artistic terms, it can effectively be seen as an implementation of counter-reformatory thought with an intent to reestablish through musical means the majesty and exaltation, the glory and greatness of the Roman Catholic Church within a framework of extraordinary liturgical celebrations. Seventeenth-century Roman polychorality, in fact, represents not only symbolically a major contribution to the Counter-Reformation in the field of composition and performance but also its 'sounding manifestation', by analogy with a great number of similar phenomena, particularly in the field of the figurative arts. From this point of view, Ballabene's Mass can be regarded as a tardy, concluding step in the history of preunitarian papal sacred music.

The author was compelled to pay a high price, in compositional terms as well as in relation to his own professional advancement, albeit against all his expectations. His work was never performed as a functional part of the liturgy – not even posthumously – but remained enchained at a theoretical, if not museum, level, limited to manuscript copies and without the (hardly practicable) publication of a printed score. This circumstance underlines once more the work's timeless nature, as a sort of rearguard in the history of the polychoral genre. This may apply at least in terms of music theory, considering the fact that Ballabene's *Kyrie* and *Gloria*, as elements of the Mass Ordinary, are functional music in name only. In light of the composer's career intentions, even the performability of the work seems to have been only one potential option from the very outset. None of this, however, can diminish the historical significance of this highly unusual work of art.

The question remains as to what should now be done with Ballabene's Mass and similar works. Burney is not known ever to have promoted either propagation or performances of the Roman polychoral works he had collected in admiration, works 'in which the learning and ingenuity ſurpaſs any thing of the kind that has come to my knowledge'. He preferred to keep them merely as an idea and cultural asset and to archive them as a part of the musical past – without either studying them or ever hearing them performed. Burney claimed that in former times 'the author of such a compoſition would have had a ſtatue erected to his honour'; well, now, owing to its exceptional qualities, Ballabene's musical monument at least has a modern edition in preparation. It will be a late tribute to this 'in every respect laudable and most difficult composition' (Martini) that – despite all its shortcomings, its inconceivableness, its being out of time – 'deserves the full approval of the first masters of the art'.

Figure 13.1 Unknown artist, portrait of Gregorio Ballabene, presumably signed by Ballabene himself (undated pencil drawing).

Source: D-B, Mus. P. Ballabene, G. I,1

Appendix I
Documents (in chronological order)

Document 1

Charles Burney on his encounter with Pasquale Pisari in Rome (1771)

Burney, Charles, *The present state of music in France and Italy*
(London: T. Becket and Co., 1771), pp. 370–372;
2nd edn (1773), pp. 381–384.

Friday 16. [November 1770] In a vifit I made Signor Santarelli[1] this morning, I found with him three or four of his brethren of the pope's chapel; among the reft, Signor Pafquale Pifari, who had with him the original fcore of a mafs in 16 real parts, which was full of canons, fugues, and imitations: I never faw a more learned or ingenious compofition of the kind. Paleftrina never wrote in more than eight real parts, and few have fucceeded in fo many as thofe; but to double the number is infinitely more than doubling the difficulties. After three parts, the addition of another becomes more and more difficult; all that can be done on thefe occafions, is to adhere to a fimple melody [371] and modulation, and to keep the parts as much as poffible in contrary, or at leaft, diffimilar motion. In the compofition of Signor Pifari, every fpecies of contrivance is fuccefsfully ufed. Sometimes the parts anfwer or imitate each other, by two and two; fometimes the fubjects are inverted in fome of the parts, while their original order is preferved in others. A century or two ago, the author of fuch a compofition would have had a ftatue erected to his honour; but now, it would be equally difficult to find 16 people who would hear it with patience, as that number of good fingers, in any one place, to perform it. Befides vocal parts in this mafs, there is a part for the organ, often on a regular fubject, different from the reft: the groundwork, upon which all is built, is *canto fermo*; and, in fome of the movements this canto

---

Giuseppe Santarelli (1716–1790), castrato singer, member of the papal chapel and in 1770 *maestro pro tempore*.

fermo is made a fubject of imitation, and runs through all the parts. Upon the whole, it muft be [372] allowed, that this work, which confifts of many different movements, and is of a very confiderable length, though it may be thought by fome to require more patience than genious to accomplifh, feems fufficient to have employed a long life in compofing, and to entitle the author to great praife and admiration.

Document 2

Charles Burney (London) in a letter to Christoph Daniel Ebeling (Hamburg) on Orazio Benevoli's polychoral works (30 March 1772)

Ribeiro, Alvaro (ed.), *The letters of Dr Charles Burney,*
vol. I, 1751–1784 (Oxford: Clarendon Press, 1991), pp. 108–112: 109–110.

Benevoli was remarkable for writing in a great number of parts. I have 3 Masses by him – one for 12 equal Soprano's – one for 4 Choirs con-[110] sisting of 16 voices – & one in 24 real parts or Sei cori. – This was composed in the beginning of the last Century upon the cessation of the plague wch then had raged at Rome. It was performed at St Peter's Church by near 200 voices, the 6th Choir was placed in the cupola of that stupendous Building, & tradition says the effects produced by such a number of parts reinforced by so many voices was [sic] beyond description & imagination.

Document 3

Gregorio Ballabene (Rome) in a letter to Giambattista Martini ([Bologna]) accompanying the score of the Mass (15 August 1772)

I-Bc, Carteggio martiniano I.030.053

M.to R.do P.re Mio Sig.^r P.ne Col.mo

Da quegli Studj, che io ho pofsuto fare a misura de miei Scarsi talenti sotto Valorosi Maestri p. lo Spazio di molti anni nell'arte della Musica, e nella Scienza del Contrapunto; dopo efsermi esercitato ed in quella Varia Tea-trale, e nella Seria, e costante Ecclesiastia p. lungo tempo, n'è venuta fuori dal mio capo vna Mefsa a dodici Cori, o Sia a Voci quarantotto. Quanto io però credeuo di riceverne qualche riputazione al mio nome, che è il miglior premio delle Persone onorate, io Sono Stato costretto a Sentire da più d'uno di questi Maestri di Cappella, e da varj avtorevoli Dilettanti, efsere vna Buffonata, vn'Impostura; che le Voci Sono Solamente quattro; che queste Composizioni Sono giuochi, e Simili galanterie.

E sebbene io avrei potuto con buoni Esempj, e con vere ragioni sostenere la mia fatica, non ho voluto farlo, considerando il poco profitto, che potevasi sperarne contro li pregiudizjj. Ma poichè mi Sono avveduto, che da questo danno ne deriua vn'altro maggiore, che i Giovani Studiosi, ed i miei Scolari istefsi, Seguendo la più comoda opinione altrui, pofsono farsi beffe, e della Composizione, e del Maestro, anzi della Scienza istefsa, che ha più luminosa meta di quella, che Costoro si figurano.

perciò mi veggo in obbligo di uscire dalla mia indolenza, e ricorrere alla Vasta Cognizione della P.tà V.ra M.to R.da; acciochè ed io, e gli altri restiamo illuminati, e Sopra la vera esistenza della pluralità delle Voci, e Sopra il merito, o demerito della mia meschina produzione. Eccomi pertanto a Sottoporre al di Lei Savio discernimento quest'Opera, che non contiene altro, che il <u>Kyrie</u> compito, tutto il <u>Gloria</u> <u>in excelsis</u>; avendo voluto lasciare a miglior penna della mia il <u>Credo</u> ad vltimazione perfetta della Mefsa. Vedrà Ella, che in qualche parte mi Sono prevalso dello Stile Cantabile. Non è già, che a questi modi abbia voluto pofporre il Serio, e grave, a cui si deve principalmente servire; ma perchè volendosi eseguire, vi fofse qualche cibo ancora p. i Stomachi moderni, e di diversa complefsione.

Io sarò Costretto egualmente, e di Seppellire questa composizione, quando non le convenga altro fine; e di produrla, allorchè si lusingafse di compatimento, o forse ancora di qualche lode p. il nuovo impegno preso, o p. aver dato la traccia alli migliori miei Posteri di Sostenerlo: nel qual Caso Supplico con vero rispetto la R. V. di condecorarla con vna benigna approvazione, e di pafsarla a cod.ᵃ illustre Accademia Filarmonica, in cui ho il grande onore di vedere ascritto il mio nome; acciò Si degni di riceverla, e di distinguerla con vn generoso gradimento del quale fornita abbia il coraggio di presentarla a piedi di qualche insigne Mecenate, che vmanamente l'accolga. E qui con vera ambizione di vbbidienza, mi protesto ofsequiosamente
Di V. R.

Roma 15. Agosto 1772:

V.mo, D.mo ed Ob.mo Serv.ʳᵉ
Gregorio Ballabene

Document 4

Extract from Martini's printed approbation of Ballabene's Mass (1774)

Martini, P. Giambattista, *Descrizione, e approvazione dei Chirie, e Gloria in excelsis del Signor Gregorio Ballabene composta in musica a 48. voci in dodici cori* (Roma: A. Casaletti, 1774; in: Heiberger, *Lettera*, pp. VII–XV: VII–VIII, X–XV).

RIcercato io infrafcritto, anche a nome dell'Accademia de' Filarmonici di Bologna di rilevare, e defcrivere le qualità, ed il merito dei *Chirie, e Gloria in exelfiis* [sic] a 48. Voci diftribuite in XII. Cori dal Signor Gregorio Ballabene Romano noftro Accademico aggregato nell'anno 1754., proccurarò [sic] per quanto mi verrà permeffo dalla mia debole capacità, di efporre il valore, e l'arte fingolare ufata dall'Autore in condurre a fine lodevole un lavoro di tanto impegno.

L'arte del Contrapunto confifte nella difpofizione di varie melodie, o cantilene contrappofte l'una all'altra, ordinate fecondo le figure muficali di diverfo valore, e di varj Tempi. . . .

[VIII] . . .

Sul fine del Secolo XVI. e per il corfo intiero del XVII. fiorirono Maeftri valorofi, fingolarmente in Roma, i quali s'accinfero all'impegno grande di comporre non folo a due, ma a tre, quattro, cinque, e fei Cori, fra' quali Virgilio Mazzocchi, Pierfrancefco Valentini, Antonio Cifra, e tanti altri; ma fopra tutti Orazio Benevoli; il quale, come fi può vedere dalle fue Opere, fi refe fuperiore a tutti per la fua mirabile condotta, non folo piena di fingolari artifizj, ma nell'iftelfo tempo naturale, facile, chiara, e dilettevole. . . .

[X] . . .

Il noftro Autore, nella teffitura della fua Compofizione, ben fondato, ed iftruito nelle regole più effenziali della fua Arte; ed infaticabile in ciò, che incontrafi di più arduo, ha abbracciata, e feguita la più giufta, e fondata opinione, artifiziofamente ritrovando il modo, che in ognuno dei 12. Cori vi fia il fuo fondamento, che ferva di Bafe alle parti del fuo Coro. Infatti nella di lui Compofizione non trovafi Coro, che da fe non reggafi feparatamente dagli altri Cori.

Inoltre full'orme dei più eccellenti Maeftri nel comporre a più Cori, ha faputo artifiziofamente fcegliere nelle fughe foggetti tanto pefati, e premeditati, che ammettono varj Rivolti, Rifpofte contrarie, del Tuono, d'Imitazione, ed altri artifizi, che nell'iftelfo tempo, che dimoftrano la fomma perizia del Compofitore, fanno conofcere altresì la fua avvedutezza nello fcegliere fi fatti foggetti, per evitare con tali artifizj quella noja, e difgufto, che in tanto numero di repliche di tutte le Parti, poteva recare agli Afcolanti un foggetto femplice non fufcettibile di tali artifizj.

Di più egli ha faputo far' ufo del fingolar modo praticato da Orazio Benevoli nelle fue compofizioni a quattro Cori, di rifolvere con grande accorgimento le diffonanze nell'ifteffo tempo da più Parti, fenza urtare in unifoni, o in Ottave di feguito, come la quarta rifoluta in terza; [XI] la fettima in fefta; e la nona in ottava; fenza del quale artifizio è quafi impoffibile, che il Compofitore in tanta quantità di Parti, poffa recare a buon termine la fua compofizione. Ha faputo anche condurre i Baffi della fua compofizione con tale avvertenza; che facendo fondamento ognuno d'effi al fuo Coro; non s'incontrino fra di loro in due unifoni, o in due ottave, nè in due quinte di feguito: e tale artifizio è tanto neceffario, che fenza efferne bene iftrutto, non potrà mai qualunque fiafi Compofitore impegnarfi ad un così laboriofo affunto.

Merita fopra tutti la più diftinta lode il noftro Autore; perchè fi è refo fuperiore a tutti gli accennati gran Maeftri, i quali ogniqualvolta (per quanto mi è noto) oltrepaffarono il numero di 16. voci difpofte a quattro Cori, tralafciarono di confervare la realità della Parti, e non ebbero punto difficoltà (forfe credendo quafi impoffibile) di far cantare all'uniffono alcune Parti di un qualche Coro con quelle d'un'altro Coro. Non così fece l'inftancabile noftro Signor Ballabene; il quale nella fingolariffima teffitura della fua compofizione, feppe, riducendola al numero forprendente di 48. voci, confervare, e mantenere efattamente la reale diverfità delle Parti. E febbene Ottavio Pitoni rinomato Maeftro di Cappella di S. Pietro in Vaticano lafciaffe un'abbozzo di una Meffa confimile a 48. voci, che favorì farmi vedere nell'anno 1753. il degniffimo Signor Gio: Biordi allora Decano de' Cantori Pontifizj, e degno Maeftro di Cappella eletto per rigorofo concorfo della Chiefa di S. Giacomo de' Spagnoli: non volle però il Pitoni obbligarfi (ficcome fece anche nelle fue compofizioni a 4. Cori) alla reale diverfità delle 48. Parti; ma fece, che varie di effe cantaffero in uniffono, ora con alcune, ora con altre [XII] Parti degli altri Cori. Di tale non conveniente licenza non ha però voluto fare alcun'ufo il noftro egregio Compofitore; dimoftrando, con mantenere la reale diverfità di tutte le 48. Parti, quanto fia grande, e fingolare il fuo talento in maneggiare un numero sì prodigiofo di Parti per tutta la fua compofizione, con tanto fuo onore ridotta a lodevole, e gloriofo fine. Ciò fervir dovrebbe d'efempio ai Giovani, che s'applicano a quefta forta di comporre; acciò non fi lafcino fedurre, ed ingannare da certi uni; i quali poco amanti della fatica, fpargono, che a più di quattro Parti non fi può comporre; e che il maggior numero di effe Parti è tutta impoftura.

Nella teffitura pofcia della fua Opera a dodici Cori il noftro Autore li ha faputo difporre, e diftribuire con fingolar Maeftria. Egli ad efempio de' più celebri Maeftri ha ufato le rifpofte dei Cori all'uniffono, o alla quinta, o alla quarta, e in alcuna circoftanza (fingolarmente di modulazione) alla feconda, alla terza, alla fefta &c., e qualche volta ancora a fomiglianza di

Contrappunto doppio; cambiando il Coro fuperiore; ponendolo nel luogo inferiore, o l'inferiore nel fuperiore; col far ufo alcuna volta anche, per maggiore varietà, delle rifpofte contrarie.

E quì merita d'eſſere avvertito, come il noſtro Autore a fine di evitare negli Uditori la noja, ed il tedio, che potrebbero generarſi negli ſbattimenti dei 12. Cori; con ogni avvedutezza ha unito ſempre due Cori per volta, che formino i ſbattimenti; e con tal' arte è venuto a sfuggire l'eccedente lunghezza, ch'era inevitabile, quando ſi foſſero formati i sbattimenti da un ſolo Coro per volta.

[XIII] Per condurre però a buon termine un lavoro di tanto impegno, egli è ſtato forzato di addottare alcune eccezioni, e licenze; ſenza delle quali non era poſſibile, ch'egli poteſſe riuſcire nel ſuo intento: tanto più che è noto, ſecondo i più celebri Maeſtri di queſt' Arte, che quanto più creſce il numero delle Parti di una compoſizione; altrettanto creſcono neceſſariamente l'eccezioni, e licenze di alcune regole; le quali, uſate con tutta la poſſibile moderazione, e non oppoſta alle prime elementari regole del Contrappunto, ſi rendono non ſolo neceſſarie, ma in certe circoſtanze anche lodevoli: come vedeſi praticato da que' valenti Maeſtri nelle compoſizioni di ſoli tre, e quattro Cori.

Egli in primo luogo ha ſaputo uſare opportunamente quell'eccezioni ammeſſe da tutte le Scuole più rinomate; ſingolarmente dalla celebre Scuola Romana dei due Secoli andati. Per eſempio, che in tante circoſtanze la Nota nera, o la ſua pauſa, che nel tempo a Cappella è la Semiminima, e nel tempo ordinario è la Croma, e la ſua pauſa, ſalva li due uniſſoni, le due ottave, e le due quinte di ſeguito. Che ſe mai gli foſſero fuggiti alcuni di queſti intervalli di ſeguito, ciò deve piuttoſto attribuirſi ad inavveduto traſcorſo d'occhio, che a volontario errore; il quale in tanta quantità di Parti è quaſi impoſſibile a sfuggirſi. Infatti pochi, e quaſi neſſun Compoſitore ritrovaſi, in cui qualcuno di queſti involontarj traſcorſi di due uniſſoni, di due ottave, o due quinte non s'incontri.

Vengono però eccettuati dalle accennate proibizioni gli uniſſoni dei Soprani, e dei Contralti praticati dall'Autore ſul fine del *Chirie*, e ſul fine del *Gloria in* [XIV] *excelſis*; perchè eſſendo tali cantilene compoſte di Note di valore di più battute, o di maggior valore delle altre, e a imitazione del Canto fermo, hanno uſato i più eccellenti Maeſtri di farli cantare all'uniſono, per ſempre più rinforzarle; acciò vengano maggiormente impreſſe nelle orecchie degli Aſcoltanti.

In ſecondo luogo egli ſi è ſervito dell'ufo dei ſalti, già da' primi Maeſtri proibiti, tanto aſcendenti, che diſcendenti di quarta alterata, o maggiore; di quinta falſa; di ſeſta maggiore; di ſettima, o maggiore, o minore; così anche di tutti i ſalti ſopra l'ottava: Unicamente però quando dalla neceſſità e ſtato forzato; e ſempre però ſeguendo l'eſempio dei Compoſitori a più

Cori, ſopra tutti dell'incomparabile Orazio Benevoli. Egli, uniformandoſi all'uſo, o ſia abuſo dei moderni, ha in qualche grande riſtrettezza troncata qualche parola, affine di dar luogo ai movimenti delle Parti: la qual licenza ſe è ſtata preſa ſenza neceſſità, e nel maneggio di poche Parti da alcuni de' Compoſitori del preſente Secolo; quanto più dovrà permetterſi, ed averſi per iſcuſabile a chi ſi è poſto al grave, e difficiliſſimo impegno di maneggiare 48. Parti.

Queſto è quanto da me infraſcritto ſi è rilevato nell'eſame fatto ſopra queſta per ogni parte lodevole, e difficoltoſiſſima compoſizione; la quale ſecondo il mio debole intendimento, merita tutta l'approvazione de' primi Maeſtri dell'Arte; e ſarà ſempre di grande luſtro e all'Autore, e alla noſtra Accademia de' Filarmonici di Bologna; la quale gode il vantaggio d'avere fra ſuoi Accademici un'Uomo così inſigne, e valoroſo. In fede di quanto ho quì ſopra eſpoſto, ho [XV] firmato, e ſottoſcritta di mia mano la preſente Approvazione.

Bologna S. Franceſco li 11. Gennajo 1774.

Fr. Gio. Battiſta Martini Minor Conventuale, e Secondo Definitore dell'Accademia de' Filarmonici di Bologna.

Document 5

Anonymous French newspaper article on Ballabene's Mass (1775), largely based on Martini's *Descrizione*

Anonymous ('M***'), 'Messe à 48 voix distribuées en 12 chœurs, composée par M. Grégoire Ballabene, Maître de Chapelle de Rome', *L'esprit des journaux* (s. l. [Liège?]), vol. IV (April 1775), pp. 198–202.

Messe à 48 voix diſtribuées en 12 chœurs;
compoſée par M. Grégoire Ballabene,
Maître de Chapelle de Rome.

Ce chef-d'œuvre a été préſenté à l'Académie des Philarmoniques de Bologne, qui, après l'avoir examiné, donna une approbation bien glorieuſe à l'Auteur, qui fut agrégé à l'Académie en 1754. On lit dans cette approbation, que l'ouvrage de M. Ballabene ſurpaſſe tout ce que nous avons eu juſqu'à ce jour, par le goût, le chant agréable & le nombre des parties.

Pour pouvoir mieux apprécier le travail de ce célebre Compoſiteur, il eſt néceſſaire de donner aux amateurs l'idée du contre-point. . . .

[199] Sur la fin du feizieme fiecle & durant le dix-feptieme, on vit à Rome de grands maîtres qui fe diftinguerent en donnant des compofitions à deux, trois, quatre, cinq & fix chœurs. On [200] compte parmi ces Muficiens, Virgil Mazzocchi, Pierre-François Valentini, Antoine Cifra, & fur-tout Horace Benevoli, des talens duquel on peut juger par les excellens ouvrages qu'il nous a donnés. Ces maîtres fe font fervi & ont inventé beaucoup d'artifices en compofant à plufieurs chœurs: mais M. Ballabene, dans fa composition à douze chœurs, a introduit un bien plus grand nombre de voix que tous ces habiles Muficiens. . . .

Inftruit des regles de fon art, M. Ballabene, a, dans la compofition de fa Meffe, embraffé & fuivi l'opinion la plus jufte & la mieux fondée, qui eft que chacun des chœurs ait pour appui fa baffe fondamentale.

[201] Il a fu choifir dans les fugues des fujets, tant pefés que prémédités, qui admettent differens renverfemens, des réponfes contraires du ton [sic], des imitations & autres artifices qui annoncent le profond favoir du Compofiteur.[2] Il a fait de plus ufage de la maniere de fauver les diffonances, dans le même tems, à plufieurs parties, fans heurter en uniffons, ou en octaves de fuite, comme la quarte fauvée en tierce, la feptieme en fixieme, & la neuvieme en octave. Sans cette invention, il étoit impoffible que, dans un fi grand nombre de parties, le Compofiteur ait pu jamais atteindre le but qu'il s'étoit propofé.

M. Ballabene a encore conduit fes baffes avec tant de précifion que chacune en particulier faifant le fondement à fon chœur, elles ne fe rencontrent pas entre elles en deux uniffons, ou deux octaves, ou deux quintes de fuites. C'étoit là le point le plus difficile, & où le Compofiteur s'eft particuliérement diftingué. . . .

[202] Ce favant ouvrage devroit fervir de guide & de modele à tous ceux qui veulent approfondir les beautés de leur art. L'Auteur a démontré jufqu'à quel point un homme de génie pouvoit porter la fcience muficale en finiffant avec gloire un travail immenfe qui offroit à chaque pas des difficultés qui, jufqu'alors, avoient arrêtés les plus grands maîtres. Il est bien à defirer que M. Ballabene faffe graver cet ouvrage, afin que tous les amateurs puiffent lui rendre la juftice qu'il mérite à tous égards.

(Communiqué par M***.)

---

2 Content not entirely congruent with Martini's text, where the passage reads as follows: 'ha faputo artifiziofamente fcegliere nelle fughe foggetti tanto pefati, e premeditati, che ammettono varj Rivolti, Rifpofte contrarie, del Tuono, d'Imitazione, ed altri artifizi, che nell'ifteffo tempo, che dimoftrano la fomma perizia del Compofitore, fanno conofcere altresì la fua avvedutezza nello fcegliere fi fatti foggetti'; Martini, *Descrizione*, p. X (see Document 4).

Document 6

Antonio Eximeno on Ballabene's Mass and Heiberger's *Lettera* (1775)

Eximeno y Pujades, Antonio, *Dubbio di D. Antonio Eximeno*
sopra il saggio fondamentale pratico di contrappunto
del Reverendissimo Padre Maestro Giambattista Martini
(Roma, M. Barbiellini, 1775), pp. 111–112.

XXX.
Natura ed origine del nostro Contrappunto
compiutamente artifizioſo.

La ſurriferita Muſica de' Bretoni dimoſtra evidentemente la verità dell'idea del Contrappunto *compiutamente artifizioſo* . . . cioè che un tal uſo dell'armonìa contemporanea, per quanto ſi ſia ripulito e riformato a' giorni noſtri, è nella ſua origine ed eſſenza barbaro: . . . ſi prenda per eſempio la Meſſa a quarant'otto parti *reali* compoſta ultimamente dal Signor Gregorio Ballabene Maeſtro di Cappella Romano; ed oſſervando il rigore della battuta ſi facciano proferire ſenza [112] cantare a quarant'otto perſone le parole del *Gloria*, come ſono ſcritte ſotto quella Muſica: ognuno può figurarſi la bella converſazione che ne naſcerà; ſono perſuaſo, che chiunque la udiſſe ſenza ſapere il fine perchè ſi faccieva, prenderebbe l'adunanza di quelle quarant'otto perſone per una gabbia di pazzi (*). La Muſica deve ſolamente aggiungere piacere ed eſpreſſione a quello, che ſi dice; ma ſe lontano dall'aggiungere eſpreſſione, mette inſieme diverſe parole, dalla combinazione delle quali ne riſultano altre ridicole, o che nulla dicono, biſogna ad onta de' noſtri pregiudizj confeſſare, che tal ſorte di Muſica è la Muſica de' Bretoni, uſata da queſti da tempo immemorabile, e nata fra di noi nella Scuola del Canto fermo. . . .

(*) Diede al Pubblico l'importante notizia della ſuddetta Meſſa in una lettera ſtampata in Roma l'anno ſcorſo uno Scolaro dello ſteſſo Signor Ballabene il quale è, a mio giudizio, più degno di lode per le ſue belle compoſizioni ſtrumentali di camera, che per l'inutile fatica di quella Meſſa. Nell'accennata lettera dopo di avere lo Scolaro ragionato profondamente per provare, che i Greci non ſapevano la Matematica neceſſaria per comporre una Meſſa a quarant'otto parti *reali* (come credo che neppur la ſappia il Signor Maeſtro Ballabene) ſoggionge *ſotto voce* queſta lepidezza: *dicaſi, ſicchè non oda il Signor D. Antonio Eximeno*. Ma il Signor D. Antonio Eximeno per udire queſte ed altre ſimili inezie, che ſi dicono ſulla Muſica greca, ha la flemma, che certamente non avrebbe per udire una Meſſa a quarant'otto parti *reali*, che fortunatamente non s'è cantata ancora, e probabilmente non ſi canterà giammai.[3]

Document 7a–b

Letter of recommendation by Cardinal Alessandro Albani, including a notarially certified list of Ballabene's merits, to support the composer's candidacy for the post of maestro di cappella at Milan Cathedral (1779)

I-Mfd, cartella 405, fasc. 27, int. 8 and 9[4]

Document 7a
SS.ri Deputati della Rev: Fabrica
del Duomo di Milano

Ill.mi e R.mi SS.ri

Concorrendo al posto, che mi ſi suppone vacante, di Maestro di Cappella di cod.to Duomo, il Sig:r Gregorio Ballabene Maeſtro di Cappella Romano, io per la particolar cognizione che ho di queſto Soggetto, che ha date molte non equivoche prove del profondo ſuo ſapere nella Muſica, lo raccomando con tutto il calore alla ſingolare bontà delle SS.rie VV.re Ill.me perchè vogliano compiacerſi di preſceglierlo al diviſato poſto; ed accludo loro un Libretto stampato, ed un Foglio autentico de' di lui requisiti, da cui potranno diſtintamente rilevare il merito del mio raccomandato. Qualora pertanto ſi degnino di conſolarlo, oltre che ho tutto il luogo di ripromettermi,

---

3 The passage in the Heiberger *Lettera* to which Eximeno refers reads as follows: 'Una delle pruove era per lui [l'Eruditiſſimo Kirckerio nella univerſale ſua Muſurgia], che [i Greci antichi] *putabant tonum bifariam dividi minime poſſe*; *hodie non tonum tantum, ſed & cujuslibet conſonantiæ proportionem algebraica induſtria* (dicaſi ſotto voce, ſicchè non oda il Sig. D. Antonio Eximenos) *irrationaliumque numerorum ſcientia fulti nullo fere negotio dividimus*' ('One of the proofs for him [the most erudite Kircher in his universal *Musurgia*] was that they [the ancient Greeks] thought that the tone could by no means be divided in two equal parts; today we divide not only the tone with scarcely any trouble, but through algebraic knowledge and based on the science of irrational numbers (*let's say it in a whisper, so that Mr D. Antonio Eximenos cannot hear it*) also the proportion of any consonance'; Heiberger, *Lettera*, p. IV).

4 The essential content of Document 7b is quoted in Torri, 'Una lettera inedita', p. 264; based on Torri's essay, it is also reproduced in Tebaldini, *L'archivio musicale*, p. 47.

che avranno a rimanere pienam.^{te} [2] contente del di lui fervizio, faranno altrefì a me un favore, p. cui refterò loro fommam.^{te} tenuto; E defiderando vivam.^{te} d'impiegarmi ne' comandi delle SS.^{rie} VV.re Ill.^{me}, mi protefto colla più perfetta ftima

Delle SS.^{rie} VV.re Ill.me

Roma 20. febbraio <u>1779</u>
Serv.^{re} di tutto cuore
Alefsandro Card.^{le} Albani

Document 7b
Requisiti
Di Gregorio Ballabene Maeftro di Cappella Romano

E' Accademico Filarmonico di Bologna

Ha la Patente della Congregazione di S. Cecilia in Roma.

Ed è Esaminatore nella medesima Città

Nel giro di varie Provincie è stato Maeftro di Cappella in diverse Chiese.

Nel Canto, e Mufica Ecclesiaftica ha fatto grandi studj; onde è provveduto di Messe, Salmi anche ad otto voci, e a Sedici eziandio.

Ha composto Drammi Serj, e Giocosi ne' pubblici Teatri

Sono suoi allievi varj eccellenti Maeftri: due de' quali trovansi in Liegi, uno Maestro di quella Cattedrale; l'altro di una Collegiata [ambedue] stati suoi Scolari nel Collegio Liegese in Roma. In questa Metropoli altri bravi Giovani hanno rifcosso pubblico applauso e nelle Chiese, e ne' principali Teatri, vantandosi de' suoi insegnamenti.

Ma la principale sua riputazione gliel'ha procacciata una Messa a quarantotto Voci distribuiti in dodici Cori; la quale fu lungamente esaminata dal celebre P. Martini, e dall'Accademia valorosa di Bologna, che ha voluto conservare Copia fra le Cose più rare; ponendo altresì il Ritratto dell'Autore fra gli Uomini illuftri di quest'Arte.

[2] L'Elogio fatto a questa Mefsa provata nella Chiesa de' SS. XII. Apostoli in presenza dell'Em.o Sig.^e Card. Alefsandro Albani, e d'infinito Popolo, che l'applaudì a piena voce, si vede stampato negli annefsi Foglj pubblicati p. gratitudine dà uno de' più bravi Scolari del Ballabene.

E' stato anche in sua gioventù valente Organista; nella qual Professione si è distinto col suonare gli Organi più grandi e difficili.

Tutte queste Cose verranno all'occorrenza autenticate: ma più di nefsuno potrà render conto del Concorrente la più volte citata Accademia di Bologna piena di egregj Maestri bastantem.^e celebri p. tutta l'Europa &c.

[second hand:]

In Nomine Domini. Amen.

Vniversiſ& Fidem facio per p.nteſ. Ego Cauſ. Cur. Cap. Notariuſ è Coll.º publicuſ infra.ptuſ qualiter per Sup.tum D. Gregorium Ballabene fuerunt Mihi& exhibita omnia, et Singula Monumenta Originalia Comprobantia Veritatem, et realitatem d. d. Requisitorum, de quibuſ Ipſe insignituſ remanet, et decoratuſ, dictaq.ᵉ Monumenta originalia diligenter vidi, et recognovi eidemq.ᵉ D. Exhibenti reſtitui, et ad hunc effectum cunctiſ et Singuliſ, ad quoſ spectat, de veritate [3] et realitate d. d. Requisitorum teſtor, ac publicum perhibeo Teſtimonium non Solum, sed et omni& In quorum fidem& Datu. Romae ex Off.º Mei& hac die vigeſima Menſiſ Februarij Milleſimo Septingenteſimo Septuageſimo nono Ind.ᵉ Romana XII. Pontificatuſ autem S.mi D. N. D. Pij Divina Providentia PP. VI. anno ejuſ quinto =

[third hand:]
Ita est Jo.eſ P.ruſ Celeſt.ⁿᵘˢ Palmeriuſ Rom.ˢ Civiſ et Cur. Cap. Ap.licaᵉ Auct.ᵉ Not.ʳⁱᵘˢ è Collegio pub.ᶜᵘˢ
de eprae.miſ [?] omnibuſ rog.ᵗᵘˢ In fide m.ᵃᵉ
Jo[anni] P[almerius]
[office seal:] IVSTVS VT PALMA FLOREBIT | I[ohannes] P[almerius] C[ollegii] P[ublici] N[otarius]

Document 8

Charles Burney on Orazio Benevoli's polychoral writing (1789)

> Burney, Charles, *A general history of music*, 4 vols. (London: T. Becket – J. Robson – G. Robinson, 1776–1789); vol. III (1789), p. 525.

Antimo Liberati, the ſcholar of Benevoli, has celebrated his [i. e. Benevoli's] uncommon abilities in the higheſt ſtrain of panegyric; telling us that he not only ſurpaſſed his maſter Bernard Nanino, but all the contrapuntiſts that had ever exiſted, in harmonizing four and even ſix choirs of four parts each, with as much facility of fugue and imitation, as if he had been only writing for one.[5] Violent praiſe, as well as abuſe, is always ſuſpicious; but being in poſſeſſion of ſeveral curious productions of this kind, by Benevoli, I can venture to affirm, that his powers of managing an unwieldy ſcore are truly wonderful; particularly in a maſs *a ſei cori*, or twenty-four voices, in which

5 Here Burney paraphrases Liberati, *Lettera*, f. 28f.

the learning and ingenuity furpafs any thing of the kind that has come to my knowledge.

I have another mafs of his compofition, for twelve *foprani*, or treble voices, in conftructing which, the nearnefs of the parts muft have augmented the difficulty of avoiding confufion. His compofitions of this kind have been recommended to musical ftudents as models of perfection, by P. Martini, and P. Poalucci [sic].

Document 9

Francesco Galeazzi on outstanding representatives of polychoral composition (1791)

> Galeazzi, Francesco, *Elementi teorico-pratici di musica,* 2 vols.
> (Roma: Pilucchi Cracas, 1791); vol. II, p. 276.

Nello scrivere a 16 si è più di tutti segnalato *Orazio Benevoli* Celebre Maestro della Basilica Vaticana verso la fine dello scorso secolo . . . ed a' giorni nostri si è veduto un portento in tal genere, cioè una Messa a 48 voci in 12 Cori distribuite, ognun de' quali da Se si regge senza bisogno degli altri; opera insigne e maravigliosa del Sig. *Gregorio Ballabene* Maestro di Cappella Romano, e che in questo genere è il maggior sforzo dell'ingegno umano fin' ora veduto.

Document 10

Johann Friedrich Reichardt, additions proposed for *Gerber's Historisch-Biographisches Lexicon*[6] (1793)

> *Musikalische Monathsschrift* (still named *Musikalisches Wochenblatt*),
> ed. Johann Friedrich Reichardt, Friedrich Ludwig Aemilius Kunzen
> (Berlin: Berlinische Musikhandlung, 1793), IX, p. 65.

1. Fortsetzung der Berichtigungen und Zusätze zum Gerberschen Lexikon der Tonkünstler u. s. w. von J. F. Reichardt.

Seite [recte: Kolumne] 102 fehlt: *Ballabene* (Gregorio), ein noch in *Rom* lebender sehr alter Kirchenkomponist, der in Italien mit dem auch sehr alten Kapellmeister *Sala* in Neapel vielleicht noch allein in dem alten grofsen

---

6 Gerber, *Historisch-Biographisches Lexicon der Tonkünstler.* Reichardt refers to vol. I. (1790), col. 102.

Kirchenstyl fleifsig und korrect arbeitet. *Ballabene* dedicirte dem Pabst *Ganganelli* eine *Messe* für 48, sage: *Acht und vierzig* wirklich gearbeitete Singstimmen *alla Capella*, die in *Rom* in der Kirche *dei santi Apostoli* mit aufserordentlichem Beifalle aufgeführt wurde, von der für mich auch schon eine Abschrift unterwegs ist. Überdem hat er sehr viele *Psalmen* für acht Stimmen mit dem *Canto fermo obligato* und mit Instrumenten komponirt. Dieser grofse Contrapunktist, dessen eigentliche Sache die Arbeit *alla Capella* ist, und der die Anwartschaft auf die Kapellmeisterstelle zu *St. Peter* in *Rom* hatte, wo nur solche Sachen gesungen werden, mufste im Jahre 1782 [recte: 1778][7] dem italiänischen Opernkomponisten *Burroni*, der in seinem Leben nichts *alla Capella* geschrieben hatte, nachstehen, und sehen, dafs dieser moderne Komponist jene ehrwürdige Stelle erhielt. Die Italiäner haben dafür das Sprichwort: *come la nostra famiglia.*

Document 11

Ernst Ludwig Gerber on Ballabene (dictionary entry, 1812)

> Gerber, Ernst Ludwig, *Neues historisch-biographisches Lexikon der Tonkünstler,* 4 vols. (Leipzig: A. Kühnel, 1812–1814), vol. I (1812), col. 244f.[8]

Ballabene (Gregorio) ein großer Kontrapunktiſt und Singkomponiſt zu Rom, geb. daſelbſt ums J. 1720, hatte ſchon ſeit 50 Jahren, wegen ſeiner außerordentlichen harmoniſchen Kenntniſſe und wegen ſeiner fleißig, korrekt und muſterhaft gearbeiteten Kirchenſachen, die allgemeine Bewunderung der Künſtlerwelt – verdient, als Hr. Kapellm. Reichardt erſt 1791 [sic] deſſen Exiſtenz entdeckte und ſie darauf im muſ. Wochenblatte bekannt machte. Ich hätte Luſt, in dem Benehmen dieſes Meiſters etwas ähliches mit unſerm verewigten Faſch zu finden: eben die unablääſſige Anhänglichkeit an Beſchäftigungen mit der Harmonie, eben dieſe ſtille Größe, dies ſich ſelbſt Genugſeyn, unbekümmert, ob es auch die Welt weiß, und wann ſie die verdiente Bewunderung zollen wird. Ballabene hat eine Meſſe, von nicht weniger als 48 würklich gearbeiteten Singſtimmen, *alla Capella*, verfertigt,

7 The staffing issue took place in 1778. Antonio Boroni (1738–1792) was master of the Cappella Giulia from 1 April 1778 to 31 December 1792, after having been officially nominated on 21 March 1778; I-Rvat, ACSP, Armadio XV, Decreti, 28, f. 120r/v (quoted in: Rostirolla, *La Cappella Giulia*, vol. II, appendix II, p. 61). For the entire context of Boroni's election, see Rostirolla, *La Cappella Giulia*, vol. I, pp. 702–704. Next to Ballabene, Boroni's further principal competitors in the application procedure were Giovanni Masi (ca 1730–after 1800) and Raimondo Lorenzini (ca 1720–1806).
8 All italicised terms in the transcription are set in Antiqua font in the original source.

ſie dem Pabſt Ganganelli dedicirt, und in der Kirche *dei santi Apostoli* zu Rom mit außerordentlichem Beyfalle aufgeführt. Wahrſcheinlich beſitzt Hr. Reichardt dieſe Meſſe nun. Die übrigen Werke deſſelben, mit denen uns Hr. Reichardt bekannt macht, beſtehen in ſehr vielen Pſalmen für 8 Stimmen, mit *Canto fermo obligato* und Inſtrumenten. Ueberhaupt arbeitete dieſer große Meiſter faſt ausſchließend *alla Capella*; und er und *Sala* in Neapel waren faſt noch die einzigen in Italien, welche in dem alten großen Kirchenſtyl korrekt arbeiteten. Im J. 1782 [recte: 1778] wurde die Kapellmeiſterſtelle an St. Peter zu Rom vakant, die einzige Kirche, in welcher noch [245] *alla Capella* geſungen wird. Ballabene, ohnerachtet ſeiner bewieſenen großen Kunſtfertigkeit in dieſem Style, ohnerachtet ſeiner wirklichen Anwartſchaft auf dieſe Stelle, ſah ſich doch am Ende von dem, in dieſer Art ganz unkundigen Opernkomponiſten, *Burroni*, verdrängt. Das gewöhnliche Loos des beſcheidenen Verdienſtes! Wahrſcheinlich iſt aber dieſer große Künſtler jetzt nicht mehr am Leben.

Document 12

Giuseppe Baini on Pisari and Ballabene (1828)

> Baini, Giuseppe, *Memorie storico-critiche della vita e delle opere di Giovanni Pierluigi da Palestrina,* 2 vols.
> (Roma: Società tipografica, 1828); vol. II, p. 65, note 513.

Pasquale Pisari romano, figlio di un povero manuale muratore, per la sua bellissima voce, onde cantava il *Merlo* all'uso de' muratori, fu raccolto da un cotal Gasperino, che insegnògli il canto: nella mutazione della voce, divenne più che sufficiente basso; vergognandosi però di cantare per un certo panico timore da cui erasi fatto vincere, tutto si dedicò allo studio della composizione, e vi riuscì mirabilmente nella scuola di Giovanni Biordi, cui aggiunse uno studio indefesso sopra le opere del Pierluigi, onde il P. Martini, in vedendo le di lui composizioni, ebbe a dire di non conoscere fra tanti compositori chi si approssimasse allo stile del Palestrina più di Pasquale Pisari, e che poteva a ragione denominarsi *il Palestrina del secolo XVIII.* . . . La corte di Portogallo per mezzo del Ministro in Roma gli richiese un *Dixit a* 16. *voci* in quattro cori reali, e tutto il servigio per l'annuale a organo a [sic] 4. voci. Con l'indefessa applicazione di più mesi compì il Pisari l'immenso lavoro: fu provato il *Dixit* nella chiesa de' SS. XII. Apostoli d'ordine dell'indicato Ministro, il quale ne fu contentissimo (in quella occasione, essendo stati invitati cento cinquanta esecutori, fu anche provato il *Kyrie, e Gloria* a 48. voci divise in 12. cori reali di Gregorio Ballabene romano, di cui il P. Martini diede alle stampe *l'approvazione ragionata.*) Inviata appena a Lisbona in due casse tutta la musica, il povero Pisari nel fiore della sua virilità cessò

di vivere mortalmente nel 1778. ed un suo nipote ancor esso manuale muratore ebbe la mercede, che finalmente giunse, di tante fatiche.

Document 13

Fortunato Santini (Rome) in a letter to François-Joseph Fétis ([Brussels]) on
Ballabene's Mass (17 February 1842)

Fétis, François-Joseph, *Correspondance*, ed. Robert Wangermée
(Sprimont: Mardaga, 2006), p. 172.

Stimatissimo Signore,

Ella ha desiderato, Signore, nella dimora fatta a Roma, che facessi copia
dell'Opera di Emilio del Cavalliere, che porta il titolo di <u>Rappresentazione
dell'Anima e del Corpo</u>; le cinque parti istromentali del madrigale <u>Altri
canti di amore</u> del celebre Monteverde. La prima commissione, sono due
mesi, che da me è fedelmente copiata nella Biblioteca Angelica; aspettavo
io che Ella mi scrivesse alcuna cosa; non vedendo i suoi caratteri ho pensato
scriverle io prima. . . .

L'è già copiata il Kyrie e il Gloria a 12 cori del Ballabene: mi permetta
che dica composizione degnissima, ma da osservarsi con attenzione somma,
non [è] da ripromettersene un grande effetto nella qualunque sia esecuzione;
perdoni questa mia forse ridicola osservazione, mi dia dunque un cenno
onde spedirla. . . .

Le cose che Ella desidera . . . io non appardo [recte: azzardo] copiarle senza
un preciso di Lei ordine: come anche le altre moltissime cose, che Ella stessa
destinò; il lavoro è grande; ed io in alcune cose avrei gran bisogno di qualche
copista, <u>che pur bisogna pagare,</u> tanto più che nella generalità sono <u>poverelli</u>. . . .

Roma li 17 febraio 1842
Via dell'Anima n° 50

e servo devoto
Fortunato Santini

Document 14

François-Joseph Fétis on polychoral writing and on Ballabene's Mass (1853)

Fétis père [i. e. Fétis, François-Joseph], 'Revue critique. De profundis',
Revue et gazette musicale de Paris (Paris), n. 27
(3 July 1853), pp. 233–235: 233f.

Toute direction de l'art a une cause. Si l'on cherche ce qui a pu conduire
les maîtres de chapelle à écrire ces compositions à plusieurs chœurs d'une
exécution si difficile, on verra que le découragement dans [234] lequel les

avait jetés Palestrina par la perfection de ses œuvres à cinq e à six voix, leur fit chercher des effets nouveaux dans l'opposition de ces chœurs placés à de certaines distances les uns des autres dans les églises. . . . Mazzocchi fit des psaumes à six chœurs; d'autres allèrent jusqu'à *huit*; enfin, Grégoire Balla- bene, musicien romain, mort en 1800 dans un âge avancé, mit le comble au luxe des combinaisons vocales, en écrivant une messe à quarante-huit voix divisées en douze chœurs, à laquelle le P. Martini a donné une approbation motivée qui a été publiée; et pourtant il est si difficile d'écrire à trois voix d'une manière élégante et pure! . . .

En 1770, la cour de Lisbonne ayant fait demander à Pascal Pisari un *Dixit* à seize voix, cette composition fut essayée dans l'église des Douze- Apôtres, à Rome, par cent cinquante chanteurs. A cette époque, rien n'était comparable à la beauté des voix de soprano et de contralto qu'on rencontrait chez les castrats; les ténors, les basses, étaient également admirables. Tous ces chantres des églises romaines étaient grands musiciens, tous savants harmonistes, et la plupart étaient des professeurs de chant comme il n'y en a plus aujourd'hui. On peut juger de ce que dut être l'exécution avec de tels artistes. Ballabene, auteur de la messe à quarante-huit voix dont j'ai parlé tout à l'heure, profita de cette circonstance pour faire essayer son ouvrage. Burney, historien anglais de la musique, se trouvait alors à Rome: il entendit cet essai, et nous apprenons de lui que, nonobstant une exécution parfaite, l'effet fut obscur, confus, et que, dans la complication de tant de parties différentes, on ne distinguait pas les rentrées des divers motifs. Il est vrai que les cent cinquante chanteurs n'ont pu fournir à chaque partie que trois exécutants environ, ce qui était insuffisant. Il n'aurait pas fallu moins de *deux mille voix* pour donner à chaque partie une accentuation saisissable. Malheur à la musique qui n'existe qu'à de pareilles conditions!

Document 15a–b

Gaetano Gaspari on Marco Santucci's sixteen-part motet *Sancta Cecilia ora pro nobis* (s. d. [ante 1881]), followed by the reasoning set out by the music commission of the Accademia Napoleone in Lucca for awarding the music prize of the academy to Santucci (1806)

Document 15a

> Gaspari, Gaetano et al., *Catalogo della Biblioteca del Liceo Musicale di Bologna,* 5 vols. (Bologna: Romagnoli Dall'Acqua – Merlani – Azzoguidi, 1890–1943); vol. I (1890), p. 95.

Trovasi questa meschina composizione in fine dell'opuscolo intitolato *Atti della solenne adunanza dell'Accademia Napoleone in occasione di celebrarsi il giorno di nascita, e di nome di S. M. I. e R. Napoleone I. il dì 15 Agosto 1806.* A pag. 21 leggesi il *Rapporto de' Giudici sul premio della Musica*, ed è a stupire come potessero maestri di grido emettere un voto così ridicolo per non dir altro, e fossero insieme cotanto poveri di scienza da non discernere il buono dal cattivo in fatto di musicali componimenti, aggiudicando poi un premio ad opera affatto destituita di qualunque pregio. In quanto al Santucci, avrebb'egli fatto meglio a scrivere a tre o quattro parti con buon garbo, che a sedici con pessimo stile e da ignorante come si dimostrò in tale suo lavoro.

Document 15b

Atti della solenne adunanza dell'Accademia Napoleone in occasione di celebrarsi il giorno di nascita, e di nome di S. M. I. e R. Napoleone I. il dì 15 agosto 1806 (Lucca: F. Bertini, 1806), pp. 21–23.

RAPPORTO DE' GIUDICI
SUL PREMIO DELLA MUSICA.

. . .

Se lo scopo dell'Accademia nel concedere il premio della Musica è quello di perfezionare l'Arte, e la Scienza dell'Armonìa, se la novità di un genere ardito di lavoro sorte [recte: sorge] senza macchia dalle infinite difficol-[22]tà, che ad ogni passo oppongono le severe leggi del contrappunto, egli è certo, che noi non possiamo ricusarci di assegnare il premio a questo insigne Mottetto. Infatti per l'eccellenza del lavoro, per la leggiadria delle consonanze, e dissonanze ben collocate, per il battimento dei Cori, dove l'industrioso artefice regola sedici voci sempre a norma della più rigida Teoria, per contenere ogni parte indipendentemente dall'altra con naturalissima cantilena, per la proporzione giudiziosa, e matematica con cui l'esperto autore distribuisce le parti, per i varj attacchi fugati, e perchè finalmente a vantaggio dell'intiera armonia ogni Coro da se perfettamente si sostiene, noi giudichiamo, che l'Autore di questa bella, e [23] sublime composizione debba meritare il Premio decretato, e gli applausi Sovrani.

Appendix II

Documented copies of Ballabene's Mass

In the course of research a large number of references regarding the existence of eighteenth- and nineteenth-century copies of the score have emerged. These documents are registered in the following list, along with the last known owner of each, plus the status quo in terms of existence and availability, including library sigla. In the case of nos. 7 and 7.1, the essential elements of both are fully complementary, and thus they seem to refer to the same document.

In the case of extant scores, detailed source descriptions have not been provided; for more specific information on the copies concerned, see the corresponding entries in the single library catalogues (consultable via rism. info, sbn.it and bibliotecamusica.it).

The physical make-up of the full scores is relatively constant at 11–12 sheets/21–23 pages of musical text. In the following entries, the page format is indicated (where known) as a significant feature of the individual item and as a criterion for identification in the event of a retrieval of presently missing copies (notably nos. 3 and 6).

A more recent manuscript copy, realised by Laurence Feininger in 1955, supposedly on the basis of the scores in I-Bc and I-Rama (nos. 2 and 11), has not been included in the following list.[1]

---

1 The copy is part of the private archive of Danilo Curti-Feininger (Trento). The manuscript, lacking the *Christe*, is dated 'finis 27 X 55'.

a. Complete copies

1. Gregorio Ballabene; personal copy   missing[2]

2. Gregorio Ballabene; officially   I-Bc, DD.109/1[3]
    submitted copy   format: 84 × 55 cm

3. Tommaso Giordani (1730/1733–1806),   acquired before 1801;
    Richard Kenrick (1781–1827)   missing since 1827[4]
                              format: 'in imperial folio' (i. e. ca 76 × 56 cm)

4. Johann Friedrich Reichardt (1752–1814)   acquired ca 1790/1791; missing[5]

5. Marchese Bartolomeo canonico   dated 1811;
    Rusconi di Cento (fl. 1830–1850)   I-Bc, DD.109/2[6]
                                                format: 106 × 40 cm

2 There is no specific reference to the existence of this copy, though it can be reasonably assumed that the composer guarded a copy of his *chef-d'oeuvre*, all the more as the Mass had not been realised as a commissioned work.

3 A comparison of the handwriting of the source with Ballabene's letters to Martini suggests that this is in fact the composer's submitted autograph score itself rather than a copy of it by an unidentified hand. The same library unit in I-Bc (DD.109) contains a second copy of the work, listed here as no. 5 (see later). Incidentally, another missing version of the Mass is the uncorrected one that Ballabene presented to Martini in his first attempt on 15 August 1772, which was returned to him in summer 1773 (see Chapter 4, n. 7). The officially submitted copy in which Ballabene's corrections were integrated was sent to Martini in October–November 1773 (see Chapter 4, n. 12).

4 Based on information collected by Sharpe (see Chapter 12, n. 9), production of the volume as early as the 1770s should not be discounted (Sharpe, 'Tommaso Giordani', p. 33; for the indication regarding the format of the volume see ibid., p. 32).

5 The initiative to order the manuscript probably came about during Reichardt's visit to Rome in 1790. For the only known references concerning the score see Documents 10 and 11. The copy that Eitner (in 1900) locates at the Berlin Sing-Akademie, an item no longer detectable today (see Fischer, *Das Archiv*), might be identical to the score coming from Reichardt's estate, whereas the copy Eitner knew at the Königliche Bibliothek seems to go along with no. 8 in this list, D-B, Mus. MS. 1070. Eitner's entry reads as follows: 'In B[ibliotheca Regia] B[erolinensi], Ms. 1070 ein Kyrie u[nd] Gloria zu 48 Stim[men] in 12 Chören, von Santini kopiert in gr[oß] fol[io]. Dieselbe als Missa 48 voc[um] in Cd. [i.e. C-Dur] P[artitur] besitzen die Singakad[emie] in Berlin. – Bologna. – Rom Cecilia.' See Eitner, *Biographisch-bibliographisches Quellen-Lexikon*, vol. I (1900), p. 316.
   Nonetheless, it remains unclear whether Reichardt ever received the copy he had ordered from Rome, as the work is not mentioned in his later writings. When his library was auctioned off in 1815, neither the score nor any other work by Ballabene was listed among its holdings, not even the Benevoli Mass he had evidently brought from Italy. The only polychoral work mentioned in this context is Fasch's sixteen-part *Kyrie* (see Reichardt, *Verzeichniß*, p. 107, n. 174).

6 Copy by an unidentified writer, bearing on the cover page the note 'Ad uſo di B. Ruſconi 1811' (or '1816'). The identification of the presumable owner as 'Marchese Bartolomeo can[oni]co Rusconi di Cento' is based on the library catalogue and may be ascribable to Gaetano Gaspari.

6.	Fortunato Santini (1777–1861)	missing (last mentioned in 1929)[7]
		format: 81 × 59 cm
7.	Bernhard Klein (1793–1832)	acquired in 1824/1825; missing[8]
7.1.	Guido Richard Wagener (1822–1896)	dated 1825; B-Bc, FOLIO-17250[9]
		format: 75 × 61 cm

7 Fellerer, *Die musikalischen Schätze*, p. 16. According to Hüntemann's catalogue of the Masses preserved in the Santini collection, Ballabene's work bore the signature '489' (Hüntemann, *Die Messen*, pp. 6, 52). Killing furthermore gives the exact measurements of the score (Killing, *Kirchenmusikalische Schätze*, p. 167). Both aspects might help in identifying the manuscript in the case of a future reappearance.

8 For the only known references concerning Klein's score, see Chapter 11, n. 22.

9 The score in Wagener's collection, copied from the Santini library ('Dalla Collezione del Signor Abbate | Fortunato Santini. Romano') and dated 1825, was acquired by the Brussels Conservatoire in 1902 as part of Wagener's music library (N. N. ['s.'], 'Die Dr. Wagenersche Musikbibliothek', p. 2). The score may possibly be identified with one of the missing copies. There is, in fact, reason to suppose that Wagener's score is closely linked to the one Klein acquired in Rome in 1824/1825, as Wagener's is dated 1825 and bears a direct reference to Santini's collection. The score itself, however, is not in Santini's hand but seems to be the work of a German writer, whereas the title page reveals itself through its design as a work of the late nineteenth century (probably added at Wagener's initiative). Surprisingly, the title reproduces exactly the same wording as the copy in D-B (including the following note added presumably by Poelchau: 'Diese Messe ist dem Pabst Ganganelli dedicirt; sie wurde in der Chiesa degli | Apostoli bei [sic] Rom aufgeführt; der Verfasser lebte noch 1782'), a circumstance that brings this score close to Poelchau's own (see n. 10).

The other presently untraceable copies can be excluded here for the following reasons:

• Ballabene's copy (no. 1 of this list) and those copied from it would hardly bear the inscription 'Dalla Collezione musicale del Signor Abbate | Fortunato Santini. Romano. | Roma MDCCCXXV'.

• The fine Giordani-Kenrick copy (no. 3), when mentioned for the last time in 1827, was bound in morocco, whereas Wagener's consists of the music sheets only, folded in half vertically.

• Reichardt's (no. 4) was acquired in the 1790s, apparently from the composer.

• Santini's copy (no. 6) is still documented as part of the Münster library holdings in 1929.

• Fétis's (no. 9) was copied only in 1842 (provided Santini did not intend to sell him an older duplicate).

• Dehn's (no. 10) was copied by Dehn himself, possibly after 1825 and without reference to Santini.

• The manuscript in I-Fc (no. 15) is catalogued as a partial copy.

8. Georg Poelchau (1773–1836)   dated 1825;
                                         D-B, Mus.MS 1070[10]

                                                 format: 74 × 52 cm[11]

9. François-Joseph Fétis (1784–1871)   copied in 1842;
                                         missing[12]

10 Poelchau's score of the Mass seems to be closely related to the one Klein purchased in Rome in 1824/1825, whereas it is clearly not the one Poelchau himself had asked Nicolai to order from Santini in 1834 (see Chapter 12, n. 3). On the one hand, cover title and inscriptions show surprising similarities with score no. 7.1. ('KYRIE E GLORIA | A XLVIII VOCI . . . ROMA MDCCCXXV'; 'Diese Messe ist dem Pabst Ganganelli dedicirt, | sie wurde in der Chiesa degli Apostoli zu Rom | aufgeführt; der Verfaßer lebte noch .1782.' The latter note added by a hand similar to Poelchau's), on the other, the score Nicolai obtained from Santini in 1835 is identifiable with the manuscript in I-Rama, A. Ms. 316 (no. 11 in this list). There is no doubt about the writer of the Berlin manuscript (D-B, Mus.MS. 1070): the score comes very clearly from Santini's hand, albeit that it shows a slightly hasty writing style, omits most section titles, uses many textual abbreviations and in some places a larger bar width (this makes the *Gloria* almost half a page longer than in I-Rama, A. Ms. 316) – possible signs of a commission prepared within a specified deadline, like for a client on a short-term stay such as Klein on his Italian honeymoon. However, Klein died (aged 39) in Berlin on 9 September 1832, whereas the copy of the Ballabene score in Poelchau's collection is mentioned before that date, in Poelchau's handwritten catalogue dated 8 May 1832 (see Chapter 11, n. 22).
     The score in B-Bc (formerly in Wagener's collection) appears to come from the professional hand of a German copyist (with some significant copying errors), though unfortunately there is no watermark or other signs to specify its provenance. It may be presumed that the score Poelchau mentions in his 1832 catalogue refers to a copy obtained from a local copyist based on the original in Klein's hands. After Klein's death in 1832 both copies might have been exchanged, allowing Poelchau to assume possession of the more authoritative Roman source (copied by Santini himself) and leaving his German copy to be passed on and eventually find its way into Wagener's collection. In that case, the Berlin manuscript (D-B, Mus.MS. 1070) would be, in actual fact, the copy Klein had obtained directly from Santini in Rome in 1824/1825, whereas the one in Wagener's collection would be the copy of Klein's score Polchau had ordered from a local copyist. This would furthermore explain why in 1834 Poelchau was still asking Nicolai in Rome to order a flawless copy of the Mass from Santini, whereas after 1836 at the latest (after Klein had passed away), there was no actual need on Poelchau's part. In September 1835 Nicolai obtained the copy from Santini, now without the necessity to forward it to Berlin, thus ending up leaving it in Rome (see Chapter 11, n. 22; Chapter 12, n. 6).
11 After having been copied the score underwent a cut at the outer and lower edges, slightly affecting Santini's staves on several pages (pp. 4–8, 14, 16). The original page format may have reached about 78 × 54 cm, the same as score no. 11 in this list, which likewise comes from Santini's studio.
12 The only document referring to this copy is Santini's letter to Fétis, dated 17 February 1842 (see Document 13). It remains uncertain whether the manuscript, whose completion Santini explicitly reports ('L'è già copiata il Kyrie e il Gloria a 12 cori del Ballabene'), was ever delivered.

10. Siegfried Wilhelm Dehn (1799–1858)

copied by Dehn himself; missing since 1858[13]

11. Otto Nicolai (1810–1849)

acquired in 1835; I-Rama, A. MS 316[14]

format: 78 × 54 cm

12. Aleksandr Jakovlevič Skarjatin (1815–1884)

acquired between 1843 and 1858; RUS-Mk, XI-442[15]

format: 72 × 61 cm

---

13 The score is mentioned exclusively in the printed obituaries as one of the musical works that Dehn had copied on his own behalf (see Chapter 11, n. 22; Chapter 12, n. 10).

14 As has been mentioned earlier, Nicolai claims to have ordered a copy of the work personally from Santini (Nicolai, *Italienische Studien*, p. 52). The copy now in I-Rama carries a corresponding entry in Nicolai's handwriting, dated 20 September 1835 and signed 'O. N.' (Figure 12.2). Only a few days after his arrival in Rome, on 6 February 1834, Nicolai was preparing a copy of Fasch's sixteen-part Mass for himself 'before I hand it over to Santini' ('ich schrieb an der Partitur der Faschschen 16stimmigen Messe, die ich mir kopiere, ehe ich sie an Santini abgebe'); a week later, on 13 February, he documented its completion (Altmann, *Otto Nicolais Tagebücher*, pp. 24, 27). Nicolai brought the Fasch to Rome either in an official capacity (on behalf of Poelchau or the Sing-Akademie, whose member Nicolai was from 1830) or on his own, but in any case it was with the intent to exchange the master copy for other works from Santini's library. Evidence shows that Nicolai came to Rome in 1834 with very specific purchase orders from his Berlin contacts (see Chapter 12, n. 3). The following year he reported to Poelchau that 'Santini for several weeks has been writing exclusively for me, and I have . . . taken possession of some beautiful compositions' ('Santini schreibt seit mehreren Wochen ausschließlich für mich, und ich habe mich . . . bereits in den Besitz manch schöner Composition gesetzt'; letter dated 18 September 1835, reproduced in Vierneisel, 'Otto Nicolai', p. 232). Two days after this communication, on 20 September, he obtained the Ballabene Mass from Santini.

Regarding Fasch's Mass, it might be added that the work, which consists of *Kyrie* and *Gloria* only, is still part of the Santini collection today (D-MÜs, Sant. Hs. 1484); the score, however, is only a partial copy in which the middle sections of the *Gloria* (from 'Laudamus te' to 'Qui sedes ad dexteram Patris, miserere nostri' [sic]) are missing.

15 On Skarjatin and his music collection, comprising the copy of Ballabene's Mass, see Chapter 12, n. 8.

16 This score explicitly indicates the year '1772' as part of the title ('Messa a 48. voci divisa in 12. Cori. Opera del | Sig.ʳ Gregorio Ballabene Romano 1772. Opera dico | mai più fatta da Uomo fino a questi anni'), but this does not necessarily reflect the year that it was copied. In

b.   Partial copies

13. Johann Simon Mayr (1763–1845); excerpts   dated 1772; I-BGc, 267.4/2[16]

format: 112 × 40 cm[17]

14. Giuseppe Baini (1775–1844); excerpts   dated 1772;
I-Rc, MS 1672[18]

format: 105,5 × 38,5 cm[19]

15. [unknown]; *Christe eleison* only   in I-Fc; missing[20]

this form, the title seems to be more of a reference to Ballabene's personal copy (or another one deriving from it), which served as master copy for the partial score in Mayr's estate. The score, entirely in an unidentified (presumably late eighteenth-century) hand, seems to have been created basically for demonstration purposes, as it contains only 'Stubs for 48 voices by Mr Ballabene from the Mass' ('Squarci a 48 voci del Sig.ʳ Ballabene dalla messa'). It is limited to the following sections of the work: *Kyrie* I (bars 1–21); *Gloria*: 'in excelsis Deo' (bars 23–29) and from 'glorificamus te' to 'gloriam tuam' (bars 61–82); in both sections the basso continuo line is incomplete. In terms of content, the score is basically congruent with the one owned by Baini (no. 14 of this list); a common master copy may be assumed.

17 The score is written on 56 × 40 cm sheets with 24 (Choirs I–VI) respectively 25 staves (Choirs VII–XII, plus organ) per page, thus consisting of one partial score for each 'half' of the ensemble. For reading, both must be placed next to each other.

18 This score is part of the Fondo Baini (former signature: O.I.26ª; not mentioned either in the twentieth-century typewritten card catalogue or in the electronic catalogue). The manuscript, entirely in Baini's handwriting, seems to have been created basically for demonstration purposes, as it contains only 'Two stubs from the Mass for 48 voices, divided into 12 choruses by Mr Gregorio Ballabene' ('Due Squarci della Messa a 48. Voci, divisa in 12. Chori. Opera del Sig.ᵉ Gregorio Ballabene Romano 1772. | Opus vere aureum' [respectively: 'Opus cedro dignissimum']). The score explicitly indicates the year '1772' as part of the title, which cannot reflect the year when it was copied (Baini was born in 1775). It is limited to the following sections of the work: *Kyrie* I (bars 1–21); *Gloria*: 'in excelsis Deo' (bars 23–29) and from 'glorificamus te' to 'gloriam tuam' (bars 61–82); in both sections the basso continuo line is incomplete. In terms of content, the score is basically congruent with the one owned by Mayr (no. 13 in this list); a common master copy may be assumed. Baini's volume, however, consists of twelve mainly empty leaves (with forty-nine staves each), which raises the question whether it was originally created to contain the entire *Kyrie* and *Gloria* by Ballabene (the score as a whole extends to twenty-one, maximum twenty-two, pages). As only 'Two Stubs from the Mass' were inserted, Baini used the third leaf to write out the resolution of the Romano Micheli nine-choir (thirty-six-part) canon reported in Athanasius Kircher's *Musurgia universalis* from 1650 ('Canone di Romano Micheli. | Riportato nel Frontespizio del Libro VII. della sua Musurgia dal P. Kirker'). The remaining pages of the volume (ff. 4–12) have been left empty.

19 To obtain this page format a similar solution as in no. 13 is used, now with the sheets glued together on the short side.

20 Mentioned in the twentieth-century handwritten card catalogue (I-Fc, E. I. 36), according to which the score is limited to the sixteen-part *Christe eleison*. According to Gmeinwieser, I-Fc possesses even a complete copy of the work (Gmeinwieser, 'Ballabene', col. 107). This information emerges from a typewritten version of the library's card catalogue; here I-Fc, E. I. 36 is described as 'Messa in 12 cori. (Kyrie e Gloria). 1774', contained in an eighteenth-century manuscript score of 17 pages. The document is presently not otherwise detectable.

Bibliography

A. W. T., 'Sketch of Prof. Dehn', *Dwight's Journal of Music* (Boston), 14/7 (13 November 1858), pp. 259–261.

Alfieri, Pietro, *Brevi notizie storiche sulla congregazione ed accademia de'maestri e professori di musica di Roma sotto l'invocazione di Santa Cecilia* (Roma: Perego-Salvioni, 1845).

Altmann, Wilhelm, *Otto Nicolai. Briefe an seinen Vater* (Regensburg: G. Bosse, 1924).

Altmann, Wilhelm, *Otto Nicolais Tagebücher* (Regensburg: G. Bosse, 1937).

Ambros, August Wilhelm, *Geschichte der Musik*, 5 vols. (Breslau-Leipzig: F.E.C. Leuckart, 1862–1882); 3rd improved edition, ed. Hugo Leichtentritt (Leipzig: F.E.C. Leuckart, 1909).

Anonymous ('M***'), 'Messe à 48 voix distribuées en 12 chœurs, composée par M. Grégoire Ballabene, Maître de Chapelle de Rome', *L'Esprit des Journaux* (s. l. [Liège]), vol. IV (April 1775), pp. 198–202.

Atti della solenne adunanza dell'Accademia Napoleone in occasione di celebrarsi il giorno di nascita, e di nome di S. M. I. e R. Napoleone I. il dì 15. agosto 1806 (Lucca: F. Bertini, 1806).

Baini, Giuseppe, *Memorie storico-critiche della vita e delle opere di Giovanni Pierluigi da Palestrina*, 2 vols. (Roma: Società tipografica, 1828).

Baini, Giuseppe, 'Mottetto a quattro cori del Sig.ʳ Maestro D. Marco Santucci premiato dall'Accademia Napoleone in Lucca l'anno 1806. Esaminato e criticato da Giuseppe Baini Cappellano Cantore Pontificio' (manuscript, dated 'X. Kal. Februarii [i.e. 23. January] anno 1808'), I-Rc, MS 2895.

Barbieri, Patrizio, 'An assessment of musicians and instrument-makers in Rome during Handel's stay: the 1708 Grand Taxation', *Early Music*, 37/4 (2009), pp. 597–619.

Bassani, Florian, 'Polychoral performance practice and *maestro di cappella* conducting', *Performance Practice Review*, 17/1 (2012), Art. 2. https://scholarship.claremont.edu/ppr/vol17/iss1/2/

Bassani, Florian, *Römische Mehrchörigkeit des 17. Jahrhunderts. Geschichte – Satztechnik – Aufführungspraxis*, 3 vols. (forthcoming).

Benevoli, Orazio, *Psalmus Dixit Dominus in honorem Sancti Thomae de Villanova XXIV vocibus concinendus in secundo tono compositus*, ed. Laurence Feininger (Romae: Societas Universalis Sanctae Ceciliae, 1950).

Berwin, Adolfo, Hirschfeld, Robert, *Internationale Ausstellung für Musik- und Theaterwesen 1892 Wien, Fach-Katalog der Abtheilung des Königreichs Italien* (Wien: Ausstellungs-Commission, 1892).

Bishop, John, Warren, Joseph (eds.), *Repertorium musicæ antiquæ, A miscellaneous collection of classical compositions* [. . .], Part I: *Dixit Dominus (Psalm) for 24 voices* [by] *O. Benevoli* (London: R. Cocks and Co., 1848).

Burney, Charles, *The present state of music in France and Italy* (London: T. Becket and Co., 1771; 2nd edition 1773).

Burney, Charles, *A general history of music: from the earliest ages to the present period*, 4 vols. (London: T. Becket – J. Robson – G. Robinson, 1776–1789).

Burney, Charles, *An account of the musical performances in Westminster-Abbey and the Pantheon, May 26th, 27th, 29th; and June the 3d, and 5th, 1784, in commemoration of Handel* (London: Musical Fund – T. Payne – G. Robinson, 1785).

Caetano [Caetani], Ruggiero, *Le memorie de l'Anno Santo M. DC. LXXV* (Roma: M. and O. Campana, 1691).

Catalisano, Gennaro, *Grammatica-armonica fisico-matematica ragionata* (Roma: P. Giunchi, 1781).

Catalogue of the music library of Charles Burney, sold in London, 8 August 1814 ([London]: [s. n.], 1814; reprint, ed. Alec Hyatt King, Amsterdam: Knuf, 1973).

Ceccarelli, Carlo, *Poesia per musica in onore di S. Ubaldo vescovo di Gubbio da cantarsi sotto i ragguardevoli auspici di sua eccellenza il sig. Carlo Odilone Fabiani conte della Valle, signor di Villanova, e contestabile dell'anno 1784* (Gubbio: G. Bartolini, [1784]).

Degli Esposti, Giovanna, 'La Galleria dei ritratti', in *Collezionismo e storiografia musicale nel Settecento. La quadreria e la biblioteca di padre Martini*, ed. Giovanna Degli Esposti (Bologna: Nuova Alfa Editoriale, 1984), pp. 36–54.

de la Fage, Adriano, 'Studj Biografici: Giuseppe Baini', *Gazzetta musicale di Milano* (Milano), IV, 37, 14 September 1845 (Milano: Ricordi, 1845), p. 159.

De Salvo Fattor, Salvatore (ed.), *Epistolario Fortunato Santini-Gaetano Gaspari. Centoventuno lettere 'armoniche' tra Roma e Bologna (1848–1861)* (Faleria: Recercare, 2019).

De Salvo Fattor, Salvatore, *La cappella musicale pontificia nel Novecento* (Roma: Fondazione Giovanni Pierluigi da Palestrina, 2005).

Diario ordinario (Vienna-Roma: Chracas, 1718–1808; between 1755 and 1797, even-numbered issues: *Diario ordinario*, odd-numbered issues: *Diario estero*).

Dixon, Graham, '"Concertato alla romana" and Polychoral Music in Rome', in *La scuola policorale romana del Sei-Settecento, Atti del convegno internazionale di studi in memoria di Laurence Feininger*, ed. Francesco Luisi, Danilo Curti, Marco Gozzi (Trento: Provincia Autonoma di Trento, 1997), pp. 129–134.

Dizionario enciclopedico universale della musica e dei musicisti, ed. Alberto Basso, 13 vols. (Torino: Utet, 1983–1990).

Donati, Ignazio, *Salmi Boscarecci* (Venezia: A. Vincenti, 1623).

Eitner, Robert, *Biographisch-Bibliographisches Quellen-Lexikon der Musiker und Musikgelehrten*, 10 vols. (Leipzig: Breitkopf und Härtel, 1900–1904).

Engelhardt, Markus, 'Santini in Rom', in *Sacrae Musices Cultor et Propagator*. *Internationale Tagung zum 150. Todesjahr des Musiksammlers, Komponisten und Bearbeiters Fortunato Santini*, ed. Andrea Ammendola, Peter Schmitz (Münster: agenda, 2013), pp. 9–20.

Eximeno y Pujades, Antonio, *Dubbio di D. Antonio Eximeno sopra il saggio fondamentale pratico di contrappunto del Reverendissimo Padre Maestro Giambattista Martini* (Roma: M. Barbiellini, 1775).

Féderov, Vladimir, 'V. V. Stasov chez l'abb. F. Santini à Rome', in *Anthony van Hoboken. Festschrift zum 75. Geburtstag*, ed. Joseph Schmidt-Görg (Mainz: Schott, 1962), pp. 55–62.

Fellerer, Karl Gustav, *Der Palestrinastil und seine Bedeutung in der vokalen Kirchenmusik des achtzehnten Jahrhunderts* (Augsburg: B. Filser, 1929).

Fellerer, Karl Gustav, *Die musikalischen Schätze der Santinischen Sammlung. Führer durch die Ausstellung der Universitäts-Bibliothek Münster anlässlich des III. Westfälischen Musikfestes in Münster i. Westf. vom 15. bis 17. Juni 1929* (Münster: Universitäts-Bibliothek Münster, 1929).

Fellerer, Karl Gustav, 'Verzeichnis der kirchenmusikalischen Werke der Santinischen Sammlung', *Kirchenmusikalisches Jahrbuch*, 26, 27, 28–33 (1931–1939).

Fergusio, Giovanni Battista, *Mottetti e Dialogi per concertare A vna sino à noue voci* (Venezia: G. Vincenti, 1612).

Fétis, François-Joseph, *Biographie universelle des musiciens et bibliographie générale de la musique*, 8 vols. (Bruxelles: Meline, Cans et comp., 1835–1844; 2nd revised edition Paris: Firmin Didot Frères, 1860–1868).

Fétis, François-Joseph, *Correspondance*, ed. Robert Wangermée (Sprimont: Mardaga, 2006).

Fétis père [i. e. Fétis, François-Joseph], 'Revue critique. De profundis', *Revue et gazette musicale de Paris* (Paris), 27 (3 July 1853), pp. 233–235.

Fischer, Axel et al., *Das Archiv der Sing-Akademie zu Berlin: Katalog / The archive of the Sing-Akademie zu Berlin: Catalogue* (Berlin: de Gruyter, 2010).

Friedländer, R[aphael], *Carl von Winterfeld's, weil. Königl. Obertribunalsrath, Musikalische Bibliothek, welche durch den königl. Commissarius in öffentlicher Auction versteigert werden soll in Berlin Georgen-Strasse No. 29 am 15. Juni 1857 und den folgenden Tagen* (Berlin: A. Bahn & Comp., 1857).

Galeazzi, Francesco, *Elementi teorico-pratici di musica*, 2 vols. (Roma: Pilucchi Cracas, 1791).

Gambassi, Osvaldo, *L'Accademia Filarmonica di Bologna: fondazione, statuti e aggregazioni* (Firenze: L. S. Olschki, 1992).

Garda, Michela et al., *La musica degli antichi e la musica dei moderni. Storia della musica e del gusto nei trattati di Martini, Eximeno, Brown, Manfredini* (Milano: F. Angeli, 1989).

Garratt, James, *Palestrina and the German romantic imagination. Interpreting historicism in nineteenth-century music* (Cambridge: Cambridge University Press, 2002).

Gaspari, Gaetano et al., *Catalogo della Biblioteca del Liceo Musicale di Bologna*, 5 vols. (Bologna: Libreria Romagnoli dall'acqua, 1890–1943).

Gay, Peter, *The enlightenment: a comprehensive anthology* (New York: Simon and Schuster, 1973).

Gay, Peter, *The rise of modern paganism* [*The enlightenment. An interpretation*, vol. 1] (New York-London: W. W. Norton, 1977).

Gazzetta universale o sieno notizie istorice, politiche, di scienze, arti agricoltura, ec. (Firenze: [s. n.], 1774–1794).

Gerber, Ernst Ludwig, *Historisch-Biographisches Lexicon der Tonkünstler, welches Nachrichten von dem Leben und Werken musikalischer Schriftsteller, berühmter Componisten, Sänger, Meister auf Instrumenten, Dilettanten, Orgel- und Instrumentenmacher, enthält*, 2 vols.: A – M/N – Z (Leipzig: J. G. I. Breitkopf, 1790–1792).

Gerber, Ernst Ludwig, *Neues historisch-biographisches Lexikon der Tonkünstler*, 4 vols. (Leipzig: A. Kühnel, 1812–1814).

Giacobbi, Girolamo, *Prima parte de salmi concertati a due e più chori* (Venezia: A. Gardano, 1609).

Gianettini, Antonio, *Salmi a Quattro Voci, a Cappella* (Venezia: F. Rosati / A. Bortoli, 1717).

Giazotto, Remo, *Quattro secoli di storia dell'Accademia Nazionale di Santa Cecilia*, 2 vols. (Roma: Accademia nazionale di Santa Cecilia, 1970).

Gmeinwieser, Siegfried, 'Ballabene, Gregorio', in *Die Musik in Geschichte und Gegenwart*, 2nd edition, ed. Ludwig Finscher (Kassel et al.: Bärenreiter, 1994–2008), Personenteil vol. 2, col. 106–107.

Grampp, Florian, '". . . benche i Maestri tal volta si prendino qualche licenza." Anmerkungen zur Guida Armonica des Giuseppe Ottavio Pitoni', *Musiktheorie*, 20/I (2005), pp. 13–26.

Gross, Hanns, *Rome in the age of enlightenment. The post-Tridentine syndrome and the ancien regime* (Cambridge: Cambridge University Press, 1990).

Heiberger, Giuseppe, *Lettera di Giuseppe Heiberger Romano Accademico Filarmonico che serve di preludio alla Descrizione, ed approvazione fattasi dall'Accademia de' Filarmonici di Bologna ad una Composizione Musicale a 48. voci del signor Gregorio Ballabene maestro di cappella Romano* (Roma: A. Casaletti, 1774).

Heuberger, Richard, 'Internationale Ausstellung für Musik- und Theaterwesen in Wien. Musik. [Teil] III. (Schluß.)', *Allgemeine Zeitung* (München), 263 (21 September 1892), pp. 1–3.

Heyink, Rainer, '"Con un coro di eco fino in cima alla cupola": zur Vespermusik an San Pietro in Vaticano um die Mitte des 18. Jahrhunderts', *Recercare*, 11 (1999), pp. 201–226.

Hoepli, Ulrico, Oppermann, Henning, *Autographen-Sammlung des Kammerherren und russischen Gesandten Baron Karl von Knorring (1810–1870)*, 437, 28–30 May 1934 (Basel: [Oppermann], 1934).

Hüntemann, Josef Albert, *Die Messen der Santini-Bibliothek*, PhD Diss. University of Münster (Quakenbrück: Kleinert, 1928).

Janitzek, Martina, 'Santini – Stasov – Skarjatin. Drei Musiksammler', in *Festschrift für Winfried Kirsch zum 65. Geburtstag*, ed. Peter Ackermann, Ulrike Kienzle, Adolf Nowak (Tutzing: H. Schneider, 1996), pp. 219–227.

Kantner, Leopold, *'Aurea Luce'. Musik an St. Peter in Rom, 1790–1850* (Wien: Österreichische Akademie der Wissenschaften, 1979).

Kandler, Franz Sales, Kiesewetter, Raphael Georg, *Ueber das Leben und die Werke des G. Pierluigi da Palestrina* [...] *Nach den Memorie storico-critiche des Abbate Giuseppe Baini* (Leipzig: Breitkopf und Härtel, 1834).

Killing, Joseph, *Kirchenmusikalische Schätze der Bibliothek des Abbate Fortunato Santini* (Düsseldorf: L. Schwann, 1910).

Kindler, Klaus, 'Verzeichnis der musikalischen Werke Giuseppe Jannacconis (1740–1816) in der Santini-Sammlung in Münster (Westfalen)', *Fontes artis musicae: Review of the International Association of Music Libraries*, 28 (1981), pp. 313–319.

Kornmüller, Utto (OSB), *Lexikon der kirchlichen Tonkunst* (Brixen: A. Weger, 1870)

Lade, John, 'Gérard, Henri-Philippe', in *The new Grove dictionary of music and musicians*, 2nd edition, ed. Stanley Sadie (London: Macmillan, 2001), vol. 9, p. 682.

Liberati, Antimo, *Lettera scritta dal sig. Antimo Liberati in risposta ad una del sig. Ovidio Persapegi* (Roma: V. Mascardi, 1685).

Lichtenthal, Pietro, 'Coro reale', in *Dizionario e bibliografia della musica*, ed. Pietro Lichtenthal (Milano: A. Fontana, 1836), vol. I, p. 217.

Liepmannssohn, Leo (Antiquariat), *Katalog einer bedeutenden Sammlung von Musiker-Autographen seit Mitte des sechszehnten Jahrhunderts bis zur neuesten Zeit*, 3–4 December 1886 (Berlin: [L. Liepmannssohn], [1886]).

Malinina, Galina, 'Santini's collection of musical manuscripts in the Taneev Library of the Moscow Conservatoire: The relationship between two cultures', in *'Sacrae Musices Cultor et Propagator'. Internationale Tagung zum 150. Todesjahr des Musiksammlers, Komponisten und Bearbeiters Fortunato Santini*, ed. Andrea Ammendola, Peter Schmitz (Münster: agenda, 2013), pp. 145–163.

Martini, Padre Giambattista, *Descrizione, e approvazione dei Chirie, e Gloria in excelsis del signor Gregorio Ballabene Composta in Musica a 48. Voci in dodici cori* (Roma: A. Casaletti, 1774; in: Heiberger, *Lettera*, pp. VII–XV).

Martini, Padre Giambattista, *Saggio fondamentale pratico di contrapunto sopra il canto fermo*, 2 vols. (Bologna: L. della Volpe, 1774–1775).

Medvedeva, I. A., Sigida, S. Ju., 'Аннотированный указатель к собранию нотных рукописей, выполненных итальянским композитором 19 века Ф. Сантини, из фонда именных колхозных библиотек консерватории' ('Annotated index to the musical manuscript collection made by the 19th century Italian composer F. Santini at the collection of collective libraries of the Conservatory'), typewritten document (Москва, 1974).

Mischiati, Oscar, 'Una statistica della musica a Roma nel 1694', *Note d'archivio per la storia musicale* (nuova serie), 1 (1983), pp. 209–227.

N. N. ['s.'], 'Die Dr. Wagenersche Musikbibliothek', *Allgemeine Zeitung* (München), 250 (11 September 1902), p. 2.

Nicolai, Otto, 'Italienische Studien. Ueber die Sixtinische Capelle in Rom', *Neue Zeitschrift für Musik* (Leipzig), 13 (14 February 1837), pp. 51–53; republished in: Kruse, Georg Richard (ed.), *Otto Nicolai. Musikalische Aufsätze* (Regensburg: G. Bosse, 1913, pp. 53–76).

Pisari, Paschale, *Psalmus Dixit Dominus (quinti toni), XVI vocibus concinendus, compositus anno jubilaei 1775*, ed. Laurence Feininger (Trento: Societas Universalis Sanctae Ceciliae, 1961).

Pitoni, Giuseppe Ottavio, *Psalmus Dixit Dominus, II (octavi toni), XVI vocibus concinendus, anno 1685 compositus*, ed. Laurence Feininger (Trento: Societas Universalis Sanctae Ceciliae, 1960).

Pitoni, Giuseppe Ottavio, *Psalmus Dixit Dominus, III (octavi toni), XVI vocibus concinendus, anno 1719 compositus*, ed. Laurence Feininger (Trento: Societas Universalis Sanctae Ceciliae, 1960).

Pitoni, Giuseppe Ottavio, *Notitia de' contrapuntisti e compositori di musica*, ed. Cesarino Ruini (Firenze: Olschki, 1988).

Pitoni, Giuseppe Ottavio, *Guida Armonica, Libro Primo* ([Roma]: [s. n.], [ca 1708]; reprint, ed. Francesco Luisi, Lucca: Libreria musicale italiana editrice, 1989).

Reichardt, Johann Friedrich, '1. Fortsetzung der Berichtigungen und Zusätze zum Gerberschen Lexikon der Tonkünstler u. s. w.', *Musikalische Monathsschrift* (still named *Musikalisches Wochenblatt*), ed. Johann Friedrich Reichardt, Friedrich Ludwig Aemilius Kunzen (Berlin: Berlinische Musikhandlung, 1793), IX, p. 65.

Reichardt, Johann Friedrich, *Verzeichniß der von dem zu Giebichenstein bei Halle verstorbenen Herrn Kapellmeister Reichardt hinterlassenen Buecher und Musikalien, welche den 29sten April 1816 und in den darauf folgenden Tagen Nachmittags um 2 Uhr zu Halle an den Meistbiethenden verkauft werden sollen* (Halle: [s. n.], 1815).

Ribeiro, Alvaro (ed.), *The letters of Dr Charles Burney*, vol. I, 1751–1784 (Oxford: Clarendon Press, 1991).

Riepe, Juliane, 'Musik im Anno Santo. Das Heilige Jahr 1650 im Spiegel der Diarien', *Analecta musicologica*, 33 (2004), pp. 101–143.

Rigatti, Giovanni Antonio, *Messa e Salmi* (Venezia: B. Magni, 1640).

Rostirolla, Giancarlo, 'La corrispondenza fra Martini e Girolamo Chiti: una fonte preziosa per la conoscenza del Settecento musicale italiano', in *Padre Martini. Musica e cultura nel Settecento europeo*, ed. Angelo Pompilio (Firenze: L. S. Olschki, 1987), pp. 211–275.

Rostirolla, Giancarlo et al., *Il 'Mondo novo' musicale di Pier Leone Ghezzi* (Milano: Skira, 2001).

Rostirolla, Giancarlo, '"Musica antica", collezionismo e biblioteche musicali nella Roma di metà '800: il contributo di Fortunato Santini', *Nuova rivista musicale italiana*, 12/1 (2008), pp. 5–56.

Rostirolla, Giancarlo, 'Riletture: Vladimir Vasil'evič Stasov. L'abate Santini e la sua collezione musicale a Roma', *Nuova rivista musicale italiana*, 12/3 (2008), pp. 335–384.

Rostirolla, Giancarlo et al., *Epistolario Giovanni Battista Martini e Girolamo Chiti (1745–1759). Settecento musicale erudito: 472 lettere del Museo Internazionale e Biblioteca della Musica di Bologna, con l'inedita descrizione della cappella Corsini in San Giovanni in Laterano di Girolamo Chiti* (Roma: IBIMUS, 2010).

Rostirolla, Giancarlo, 'Passione per la musica antica e collezionismo. Vladimir Stasov e l'abate Fortunato Santini a Roma', in *Musicologia come pretesto. Scritti in memoria di Emilia Zanetti*, ed. Tiziana Affortunato (Roma: Istituto italiano per la storia della musica, 2011), pp. 415–454.

Rostirolla, Giancarlo, *La Cappella Giulia 1513–2013. Cinque secoli di musica sacra in San Pietro*, 2 vols., (Kassel et al.: Bärenreiter, 2017).

Ruggieri [Ruggeri], Giovanni Simone, *Diario Dell'Anno del Santiss. Giubileo M. D. C. L. Celebrato in Roma dalla Santità di N. S. Papa Innocentio X* [. . .] *Da Gio: Simone Ruggeri Romano* (Roma: F. Moneta, 1651).

Scheideler, Ullrich, *Komponieren im Angesicht der Musikgeschichte. Studien zur geistlichen a-capella-Musik in der ersten Hälfte des 19. Jahrhunderts im Umkreis der Sing-Akademie zu Berlin* (Berlin: MBV, 2010).

Scholz, Bernhard, 'Siegfried Wilhelm Dehn. Nekrolog', *Niederrheinische Musik-Zeitung für Kunstfreunde und Künstler* (Köln), 21 (22 May 1858), pp. 161–163.

Schütz, Heinrich, *Psalmen Davids* (Dresden: G. Berg, 1619).

Sharpe, Richard, 'Tommaso Giordani, Gregorio Ballabene's Messa a dodici cori con organo and Sacred Music in Late-Eighteenth-Century Dublin', *Journal of the Society for Musicology in Ireland*, 11 (2015–2016), pp. 25–35.

Stargardt, J[oseph] A[braham], *Autographen: Literatur und Wissenschaft, Geschichte, Kunst*, 261, 8 September 1926 (Berlin: [J. A. Stargardt], 1926).

Stargardt, J[oseph] A[braham], *Autographen: Literatur, Wissenschaft, bildende Kunst, Musik, Geschichte, Kirche*, 271, 23 September 1927 (Berlin: [J. A. Stargardt], 1927).

Stargardt, J[oseph] A[braham], *Die Autographen-Sammlung Alexander Meyer Cohn's: Versteigerung in Berlin*, vol. II, 5–10 February 1906 (Berlin: [J. A. Stargardt], 1906).

Tebaldini, Giovanni, *L'archivio musicale della Cappella Antoniana in Padova: illustrazione storica-critica* (Padova: Tipografia e libreria Antoniana, 1895).

Torri, Luigi, 'Una lettera inedita del Padre Giambattista Martini', *Rivista Musicale Italiana*, 2 (1895), pp. 262–286.

Verzeichniss der von dem verstorbenen Grossh. Badischen Prof. der Rechte und Geheimenrathe Dr. Anton Friedrich Justus Thibaut zu Heidelberg hinterlassenen Musikaliensammlung, welche als ein Ganzes ungetrennt veräussert werden soll (Heidelberg: K. Groos, 1842).

Viadana, Lodovico Grossi da, *Salmi à quattro Chori* (Venezia: G. Vincenti, 1612), Basso Generale, preface ('Modo di concertare i detti Salmi a quattro chori.')

Vierneisel, Wilhelm, 'Otto Nicolai als Musiksammler', in *Festschrift Max Schneider zum 80. Geburtstage*, ed. Walther Vetter (Leipzig: Deutscher Verlag für Musik, 1955), pp. 227–240.

Vogler, Georg Joseph, *Betrachtungen der Mannheimer Tonschule. Zweyten Jahrganges Neunte und zehnte Lieferung* ([Speyer], [s. n.], 1780).

Wartenegg, Felix von, 'Die Wiener internationale Ausstellung für Musik und Theaterwesen', *Neue Zeitschrift für Musik* (Leipzig), 20 (18 May 1892), pp. 225–227.

Wichmann, H[ermann], 'Das größte Musik-Kunststück der Welt', *Allgemeine Zeitung* (München), 77 (18 March 1886), pp. 1130–1131.

Wörmann, Wilhelm, [Catalogue of the Santini collection], (typewritten, ante 1957).

Index

For Product Safety Concerns and Information please contact our EU
representative GPSR@taylorandfrancis.com Taylor & Francis Verlag GmbH,
Kaufingerstraße 24, 80331 München, Germany

Printed and bound by CPI Group (UK) Ltd, Croydon, CR0 4YY
11/04/2025
01844011-0006